SideKick

P9-DHI-053

Borland's No-Nonsense License Statement!

This software is protected by both United States copyright law and international treaty provisions. Therefore, you must treat this software *just like a book*, with the following single exception. Borland International authorizes you to make archival copies of the software for the sole purpose of backing-up our software and protecting your investment from loss.

By saying, "just like a book," Borland means, for example, that this software may be used by any number of people and may be freely moved from one computer location to another, so long as there is **no possibility** of it being used at one location while it's being used at another. Just like a book that can't be read by two different people in two different places at the same time, neither can the software be used by two different people in two different places at the same time. (Unless, of course, Borland's copyright has been violated.)

WARRANTY

With respect to the physical diskette and physical documentation enclosed herein, Borland International, Inc. ("Borland") warrants the same to be free of defects in materials and workmanship for a period of 60 days from the date of purchase. In the event of notification within the warranty period of defects in material or workmanship, Borland will replace the defective diskette or documentation. **If you need to return a product, call the Borland Customer Service Department to obtain a return authorization number.** The remedy for breach of this warranty shall be limited to replacement and shall not encompass any other damages, including but not limited to loss of profit, and special, incidental, consequential, or other similar claims.

Borland International, Inc. specifically disclaims all other warranties, expressed or implied, including but not limited to implied warranties of merchantability and fitness for a particular purpose with respect to defects in the diskette and documentation, and the program license granted herein in particular, and without limiting operation of the program license with respect to any particular application, use, or purpose. In no event shall Borland be liable for any loss of profit or any other commercial damage, including but not limited to special, incidental, consequential or other damages.

GOVERNING LAW

This statement shall be construed, interpreted, and governed by the laws of the state of California.

BOR 0181

Fold at dotted line. Tape closed. Drop in mail. No postage necessary.

2

READ ME FIRST

In order to provide you with the latest technical information on our products, announcements of future updates, and up-to-the-minute information on new products, please complete and return this registration form. Be sure to read the Borland No-Nonsense License Statement on the other side.

Technical Support—To receive telephone technical support, you must be a registered owner of the Borland product about which you are calling. Prompt technical support is available through the Borland SIG on CompuServe; just type GO BOR at any CompuServe prompt. If you need further assistance, call Borland and be prepared to give the product name, version number, and the serial number found on the label of your master diskette.

The README File—If present on your master diskette, this file contains important information that may not be in the manual. To view this file, simply type README at the command prompt. Be sure to read this file before you call for technical support.

Thank you for completing this product registration card and returning it promptly. We want to keep you informed.

Product Name: _____ Serial # _____-_____-_____ Date Purchased: ___/___/___
                                                                                        M   D   Y.

Name: _____ Title: _____
        last   first   middle init.

Company Name: _____ Department: _____

Address: _____ Mail Stop: _____

City: _____ State: _____ Zip: _____ Country: _____ Phone # (_____) _____-_____

I have read and agree to the terms of the Borland No-Nonsense License Statement

Signature _____ Date: ___/___/___

In order to help us better serve your needs, please complete the following:

Nature of your business or occupation:
1. ☐ health   2. ☐ manufacturing   3. ☐ business   4. ☐ programming
5. ☐ construction   6. ☐ retail/wholesale   7. ☐ services   8. ☐ education
9. ☐ legal   10. ☐ consulting   11. ☐ finance   12. ☐ transportation
13. ☐ government   ☐ other _____

Number of employees:
1. ☐ 1-24   2. ☐ 25-99   3. ☐ 100-499   4. ☐ 500-1999   5. ☐ 2000-9999   6. ☐ more than 9999

Number of PCs at your business:
1. ☐ 1-9   2. ☐ 10-49   3. ☐ 50-249   4. ☐ 250-999   5. ☐ more than 999

What other Borland products do you own?
1. ☐ Turbo Pascal   2. ☐ Pascal Toolboxes   3. ☐ SideKick
4. ☐ SuperKey   5. ☐ Reflex   6. ☐ Traveling SideKick
7. ☐ Turbo Lightning   8. ☐ Turbo Prolog   ☐ other

Where did you purchase this program?
1. ☐ Borland mail order   2. ☐ other mail order   3. ☐ full-service retailer
4. ☐ discount retailer   ☐ other _____

What hardware peripherals do you use?
1. ☐ modem   2. ☐ hard disk   3. ☐ EGA card
4. ☐ dot matrix   5. ☐ plotter   6. ☐ mouse _____

This software was bought for:
1. ☐ self   2. ☐ company I work for   3. ☐ company I own

Where will you use this program?
1. ☐ at home   2. ☐ at work   ☐ other _____

Where did you hear about this program?
1. ☐ ad in computer publication   2. ☐ product review   3. ☐ retailer
4. ☐ ad in general interest publication   5. ☐ trade show   6. ☐ another user
   ☐ other _____

What other software do you use?
1. ☐ spreadsheet   2. ☐ database   3. ☐ word processor   4. ☐ utilities
5. ☐ project mgmt.   6. ☐ communications   7. ☐ games   8. ☐ languages
9. ☐ accounting   10. ☐ network   11. ☐ business graphics 12. ☐ CAD/CAM
13. ☐ RAM-resident utilities   ☐ other _____

What software would you consider buying from Borland?
1. ☐ spreadsheet   2. ☐ database   3. ☐ word processor   4. ☐ utilities
5. ☐ project mgmt.   6. ☐ communications   7. ☐ games   8. ☐ languages
9. ☐ accounting   10. ☐ network   11. ☐ business graphics 12. ☐ CAD/CAM
13. ☐ RAM-resident utilities   ☐ other _____

BOR0045B

SIDEKICK

Owner's Handbook

TABLE OF CONTENTS

LIST OF FIGURES

LIST OF TABLES

Notes:

INTRODUCTION

This is Sidekick

Sidekick is a lot of things, but first and foremost **it is always there when you need it**. That's because it is right there in your computer's memory all the time until you turn the power off or reset your machine. No matter which other program you are using—word processor, data base, spreadsheet, TURBO Pascal, BASIC, or whatever—Sidekick is always present 'underneath' it and may be activated immediately with a single keystroke. What's more: your other program continues as if nothing happened when you return from Sidekick.

In short, Sidekick adds a new dimension to your computer—and to your daily work, even to your life if you are a heavy computer user. It helps you organize your work and keeps your desk free of the eternal pile of paper notes, pencils, hand-calculators, phone-directories, and the whatnot that gets lost all the time anyway. You work smarter; you work easier.

Notepad
A full-screen, WordStar/TURBO Pascal compatible text editor. It includes automatic word wrap and special notepad features like *cut and paste*. It will even time and date stamp your notes —automatically if you want.

Calculator
This is a normal, everyday business pocket calculator which appears on your screen. However, it also offers special features for programmers.

Calendar
This is a perpetual calendar. With it, you can keep track of your daily appointments.

Dialer
This automatic dialer takes numbers from its own phone directory **or picks them directly off the screen**. You may find the number with dBASE III or any other database that you already own, and Sidekick will make the call!

ASCII table

When you want to see the full 256 character ASCII alphabet in decimal and hexadecimal values, with their corresponding IBM PC characters and mnemonics—it's right here. Simply a must for any programmer.

Help

When you need a helping hand, here it is—on line, and whenever convenient.

Setup

Sidekick's various standard values may be changed to suit your needs, whenever you want—no complicated installation procedures necessary!

Sidekick makes full use of windows: each function uses its own separate window, and many windows may be present on the screen at the same time. When a window opens, it will cover some other information, but everything is still present underneath it:

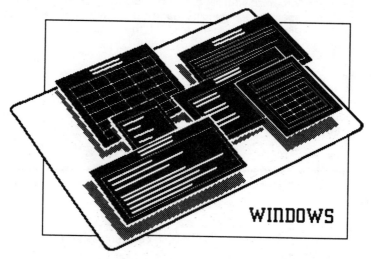

Each window may be easily moved around on the screen to uncover information that you need to see on the original screen or in other windows. The size of the Notepad window may even be varied, both horizontally and vertically—it can take up the whole screen, or just part of a line.

How to Use Sidekick

Sidekick is so easy to use that you almost don't need this handbook. On the other hand, we have written it to help you get the most out of Sidekick, and to give you inspiration about the countless ways you may use it.

Chapter 1 will tell you how to make a working copy of Sidekick and how to get it running safely. It is obviously important that you read this chapter.

We suggest you then get hands-on experience by following the short course in Chapter 2. That will make you familiar with Sidekick's main features.

Once you get going, you may want detailed information on one thing or another. You can then turn to the remaining chapters which describe each Sidekick window in detail.

Appendix A contains some ideas about the many ways you can use Sidekick. You may find inspiration there for some uses we haven't even thought of. But don't limit yourself—use your imagination!

Appendix B steps you through the installation of Sidekick—should it be necessary. In most cases it won't because Sidekick comes pre-installed to run on IBM PC's and compatibles.

Appendix C offers solutions to the problems that are most likely to arise. Please check this appendix before calling our technical support staff.

Acknowledgments

Throughout this book, reference is made to a number of trademarks: *dBase III* and *Framework* are trademarks of Ashton-Tate. *TURBO Pascal*, *SuperKey* and *Sidekick* are trademarks of Borland International Inc. *Smartmodem* is a trademark of Hayes Microcomputer Products, Inc. *Hercules* is a trademark of Hercules Computer Technology. *IBM* and *PC-DOS* are trademarks of International Business Machine Corp. *Lotus 1-2-3* and *Symphony* are trademarks of Lotus Development Corp. *WordStar* is a trademark of MicroPro International Corp. *VOAD* is a trademark of VOAD Systems.

We wish you all the best of luck with your new sidekick.

Chapter 1
GETTING STARTED

This chapter contains the information you need to get Sidekick running safely, to make work disks, etc.

Before Use

Copy-protected Sidekick

If you have the copy-protected version of Sidekick, the original disk must always be in one of your floppy drives when you start the program. Therefore, for your own protection, please make a backup copy of all the files on the distribution disk before you use Sidekick. Do **not** use a track-by-track copy program, like DISKCOPY, but a file copying program, like COPY, to copy the files onto your backup disk. Assuming that you have your backup disk in drive A: and the original disk in drive B:, you should type:

```
COPY B:*.* A: ⏎
```

to transfer Sidekick to your backup disk.

If you have a fixed disk, you might want to set up a sub-directory for Sidekick, for example one called **\SK**. First make sure that you are logged on the fixed disk (usually drive C:). You should see the prompt:

```
C>
```

If not, type C: ⏎ to log on to the fixed disk. Then type:

```
MKDIR \SK ⏎
```

Insert the distribution disk in the floppy drive, change to the \SK directory, and copy all Sidekick files to the fixed disk. Type:

```
CHDIR \SK ⏎
COPY A:*.* ⏎
```

Now store the backup disk in a safe place. In this way you will always have an uncorrupted copy of Sidekick, should anything happen to your original disk.

Non copy-protected Sidekick

Before using Sidekick, for your own protection, please copy all the files on the distribution disk onto your work disk. You should use a file copying program (*COPY*) to copy the Sidekick files onto your hard disk or floppy work disk. Assuming that you have your work disk in drive A: and the original disk in drive B:, you should type:

```
COPY B:*.* A: ⏎
```

to transfer Sidekick to your work disk.

If you have a fixed disk, you might want to set up a sub-directory for Sidekick, for example one called **\SK**. First make sure that you are logged on the fixed disk (usually drive C:). You should see the prompt:

```
C>
```

If not, type C: ⏎ to log on to the fixed disk. Then type:

```
MKDIR \SK ⏎
```

Insert the distribution disk in the floppy drive, change to the \SK directory, and copy all Sidekick files to the fixed disk. Type:

```
CHDIR \SK ⏎
COPY A:*.* ⏎
```

Now store the distribution diskette in a safe place. In this way you will always have an original, uncorrupted copy of Sidekick, should anything happen to your work disk.

Please note that Borland's no-nonsense license statement printed in the front of this book licenses you to use your copy of Sidekick as if it were a book. It is not licensed to a single person, nor is it tied to one particular computer.

The only restriction on its use is that **it must not be used by two different people at the same time**, exactly as a book cannot be read by two people at the same time. And, of course, giving away copies of it to others will be a violation of Borland's copyrights—*just like a book.*

Files on Your Diskette

In addition to the full Sidekick system, the distribution diskette contains various limited configurations which allow you to preserve memory by sacrificing some functions which you feel you can do without. This may be necessary on systems with limited memory capacity because Sidekick, like the operating system, stays in memory and thus reduces the memory available for other programs.

These files are on your disk:

SK.COM
The full Sidekick system with all features included.

SKN.COM
This system leaves out the caLendar. It keeps in the Notepad, Calculator, Dialer, and ASCII table.

SKC.COM
This system leaves out the Notepad. It keeps in the caLendar, Calculator, Dialer, and ASCII Table.

SKM.COM
This is the smallest configuration. It leaves out the Notepad, caLendar, and Dialer, and keeps only the Calculator and ASCII table.

You need only have the one system you want to use present on your work-disk.

It is a good idea to use the full system for starters. If you then run into memory problems, you may either add more memory to your computer or use one of the limited systems.

Throughout this manual we assume that you are using the full system. In the limited versions, some windows may look slightly different because of the features we've kept out.

In addition to the various versions of Sidekick, the following files are on your disk:

SK.HLP

Contains the Sidekick help texts. This file may be left off your diskette when running Sidekick if you don't want to use the built-in help. If you want to use the help system, this file must be on the disk and directory from where you start Sidekick.

SKINST.COM

This is the installation program which lets you choose screen type, define the port to be used for the modem, change Sidekick's colors, and alter the Notepad editor's commands. The use of this program is entirely optional, because we have already included all the commonly used values within Sidekick's Setup function.

READ-ME.SK

If present, this file contains the latest information on Sidekick.

You only need ONE file present on your work disk in order to activate Sidekick: the SK.COM file (or SKN.COM, SKC.COM, or SKM.COM, if you use a limited system). Once Sidekick is active, even this file is no longer needed on your disk.

Installation

Sidekick comes installed for an IBM PC computer, and it is only necessary to go through the installation procedure if you are not satisfied with the pre-set values, or if you want to use Sidekick's 'Rolodex' Dialer.

Appendix B contains all the information you need to install Sidekick.

When to Start Sidekick

Sidekick is a *resident program,* which means that it is loaded into memory and stays there until you switch off the computer. Sidekick is therefore running even while you run other programs such as a word processor or a spreadsheet.

Sidekick may not be the only resident program you use on your computer; programs such as print spoolers, RAM disks, and keyboard enhancers (Borland's *SuperKey,* for example) are other examples of resident programs. If you use any of these, it is essential that you load them in the following order:

1) Load any non-Borland resident programs **first** (print spoolers, RAM-disks, or what have you).

2) If you have SuperKey, load it **after** any non-Borland resident programs.

3) Finally load *Sidekick* as the **last** resident program.

Where to Start Sidekick From

If you use a tree-structured directory, it is important that you change to the directory where you keep Sidekick's .COM and .HLP files before you start Sidekick.

This is because Sidekick must know where to find these files when you save a Sidekick setup, or when you use the on-line help system.

If you have your Sidekick files in the directory **SK**, and all your other programs in one called **SYSTEM**, you could set up a DOS *path* which would allow you to call Sidekick from any directory. **Don't** do that with Sidekick. You **must** be on the directory that contains Sidekick's .COM and .HLP files when you start it, or you cannot save setups or use the help system.

If you use an AUTOEXEC.BAT file to set up your computer automatically each time you turn it on, please see page 87 for instructions.

Finally—Start Sidekick

Once you have Sidekick ready on your work-disk, type:

[S] [K] [↵]

to start it. The only file required on your disk at this point is SK.COM (or one of the other Sidekick .COM files, if you use a limited system). Please be sure to follow the instructions above on loading Sidekick with other resident software.

Please note that when starting the copy protected version of Sidekick, the original distribution disk must be in one of your floppy drives. Once Sidekick is started, this disk can be removed. The SK.COM file you use may be on another disk (a work disk or a fixed disk, for example).

The following message will tell you that Sidekick is now loaded into memory and working:

```
 SideKick           Version 1.5
                    IBM-PC/XT/AT/PCjr


 Copyright (C) 1984,85 BORLAND Inc.
```

```
 Full System

 524288 bytes total memory
 412896 bytes were free
 348224 bytes free
```

Figure 1-1: Log-On Message

After the copyright notice, version number, etc., a description of the Sidekick system follows. If you are running a limited version, it tells you which features are included.

The last three lines contain information about your PC's memory. First you can see how much memory you have in total, followed by the memory available after DOS and other system stuff (buffers, drivers, spoolers, RAM disks, or what have you).

The last line shows the amount of memory left after Sidekick was loaded. If this last figure is less than you need for your application program, you must either add more memory or use one of the limited Sidekick systems.

Remember that if the documentation for your software says that it requires a minimum of 128K (128 kilobytes) it normally means 128K *total* memory, **not** 128K *free* memory. As DOS and various system utilities, buffers, etc. use anywhere from 25K and upwards, it is difficult to say how much *free* memory is really needed to run that particular software. If you're in doubt, just try it.

Although Sidekick is working, you can't see it. You must press special keys, as described in the next chapter, to get in touch with Sidekick.

You can now use your computer as usual. The only difference is that Sidekick is sitting there, waiting for you to call.

The following chapter takes you on a ride with your Sidekick. Spend a little time with it—enjoy the scenery—and you'll see that you have found yourself a great new friend.

How To Stop Sidekick

One last thing before you get going. Even though Sidekick is meant to stay in your computer's memory from now on (so it's always ready to pop up at the touch of a key), special circumstances may arise where you need to remove Sidekick from memory. For instance, you may need to free the memory it occupies to create more room for other programs.

You **can** do that, but **only** when there are **no other programs** in memory **after** Sidekick.

That means that you must be certain that Sidekick is the **last** resident program you load, as described above.

Secondly, you must only remove Sidekick from memory when you are at the DOS prompt, for example:

A>

If you remove Sidekick when other programs occupy memory above it, you will create an unoccupied 'hole' in the middle of memory, and DOS will go bananas!

Observing these precautions, you can press `Ctrl` `Alt` to get Sidekick's main selection window, and then press:

`Ctrl` `Home` `End`

That means: hold down `Ctrl` and then press `Home` and `End`.

Please be sure to save your Notepad file before removing Sidekick from memory, or you'll lose its contents.

If you removed Sidekick from memory, please re-load it as described on page 10 before you continue.

Chapter 2
TAKE YOUR SIDEKICK FOR A RIDE

Activate Sidekick

If you have followed the instructions in Chapter 1, Sidekick is now loaded into memory. It stays there until you either turn off the computer or reset it.

You may use the computer exactly as usual; fire up your spreadsheet, word processor, TURBO Pascal, or even BASIC (disk BASIC, that is), and go to work. **Anytime** you need Sidekick, just press:

Ctrl   Alt

which means: hold down the Ctrl and Alt keys at the same time. Another way to call Sidekick is to hold down both △ keys. The Sidekick main selection window now pops up in the middle of the screen:

```
┌─ SideKick Main Menu ─┐
│                      │
│  F1    Help          │
│  F2    NotePad       │
│  F3    Calculator    │
│  F4    caLendar      │
│  F5    Dialer        │
│  F6    Ascii-table   │
│  F7    Setup         │
│  Esc   exit          │
│                      │
└──────────────────────┘
```

Figure 2-1: Sidekick Main Selection Window

You may now select the window you want to use in one of three ways:

1) Enter the highlighted capital letter in the window name (in either upper or lower case, or with the Alt key depressed).

2) Press the function key associated with the desired window (F1 through F7 on a full system).

3) Use the arrows to move the horizontal bar to the name of the desired window and press ⏎.

We recommend the first method, with the Alt key depressed, for reasons we will explain later.

If you press the Esc key, you return to whatever you were doing before activating Sidekick.

Help

As this is the first time you have activated Sidekick, the horizontal bar points at Help. If you press Alt , the Help window will open:

```
┌─────────────────────────────────────────────────┐
│              SIDEKICK HELP SYSTEM                │
│                                                  │
│  This  is some general information about  Sidekick. │
│  It is several pages long,  and you page through it │
│  with the ↑ and ↓ keys.  You can terminate the help │
│  at  any point by pressing the Esc-key.  Note that │
│  NumLock must not be active for the arrows to work. │
│                                                  │
│  You get detailed help on each Sidekick window when │
│  you are in a window and press F1 or Alt-H. More.._ │
│  ──────────◀ Press Esc to exit help ▶──────────  │
└─────────────────────────────────────────────────┘
```

Figure 2-2: Help Window

The help you get here is general help about using Sidekick. It is several pages long, and you page through it with the ↓ and ↑ keys. When you open a window, the context-sensitive help system will give you detailed help on whatever you are currently doing.

You exit the help text by pressing the **Esc** key.

The Esc key is used throughout Sidekick to exit whatever you are currently doing and return you to your previous activity. Esc will also close the window as you leave.

Since Help is the only window open at this point, [Esc] will return you to the outside world, i.e. to the program you were using when you activated Sidekick. Press [Ctrl][Alt] again, and you are back to the main selection window.

A Note On Graphic Displays

Sidekick always uses the screen's *text mode*. If you are displaying graphics on the screen when you activate Sidekick, it will turn into scattered blots of strange characters in different colors, and Sidekick will appear on top of this. Not to worry. When you exit Sidekick, your graphics will return.

The Hercules and compatible adapters present special problems, as they handle graphics differently from the IBM standard. Sidekick does its best to determine the type of hardware in your computer and handle it properly.

Some boards which claim to be Hercules compatible, however, may not be 100% so, and Sidekick may not recognize it. If your card is not truly compatible, your monitor may remain in graphics mode when Sidekick is activated, or your monitor may remain in text mode after you exit from Sidekick. In either case, you should avoid activating Sidekick when your display is in graphics mode.

Move Sidekick's Windows

With the main selection window on the screen, press [Scroll Lock] to activate *ScrollLock*. Notice the message *ScrollLock* that appears at the lower right corner of the screen. It tells you that [Scroll Lock] is active. Also make sure that [Num Lock] is not active.

Now play with the cursor control keys [←] [↑] [↓] and [→] These move the window around on the screen.

This works anywhere in Sidekick. If the window in current use is obscuring some information underneath it, you can activate [Scroll Lock] and move the window with the cursor control keys.

If you want to make the new window position permanent, you must press [Alt][S] to activate the *Setup* window and then *Save* your window setup (see page 86 for details).

Notepad

Now open the Notepad window. You may press 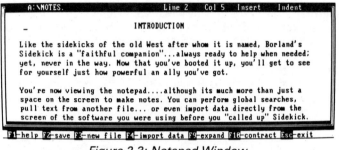, ,Alt N ,
F2 , or move the bar with the arrows and press ⏎ . We
recommend pressing Alt N (N should remind you of **N**otepad, so
it's easy to remember).

The Notepad appears at the bottom of the screen:

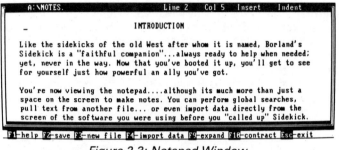

Figure 2-3: Notepad Window

The bottom line of the screen is the Sidekick *command line* which is
where you can always see which function keys are available, and
what they do. F1 gives you on-line help on the Notepad; we'll look
at the others below.

The top line of the Notepad window is the *status line* and shows the
name of the note file you are currently using, tells you where you are
in the file, and displays the status of some of Notepad's features. You
need not pay too much attention to all that right now.

You may now enter your text. Notepad is completely compatible
with the *TURBO Pascal* editor, and almost identical to *WordStar.* If
you know either of these editors, you only need to read pages 63 and
66, which explain differences and extensions.

Otherwise, here's a quick rundown of what to do:

To write: Enter your text as you would on a typewriter. When you
reach the bottom of the window, the text 'scrolls' upwards, and the
top line disappears from the window—but don't worry, it is not lost.

To move: You may move the cursor freely within the window using the arrows on the numeric keypad, and the [PgUp] and [PgDn] keys scroll the page up and down, one windowful at a time.

Remember that the arrows and the other function keys on the numeric keypad only work when [Num Lock] is not active. Normally, the state of this key cannot be seen. In Sidekick, you can see the status of both [Num Lock] and [Scroll Lock] in the lower right corner of the screen. A few Sidekick commands may be obscured by the status message; if that happens just press [Num Lock] or [Scroll Lock], and the text underneath appears.

To delete: You delete characters to the left of the cursor with the [←] key and to the right of the cursor with the [Del] key. Entire words to the right are deleted by pressing [Ctrl][T], i.e. you hold down the [Ctrl] key and then press [T]. Entire lines are deleted with [Ctrl][Y].

To insert: Characters are normally inserted into the existing text whenever you write in the middle of a line. If you press the [Ins] key, you switch to *Overwrite* mode, as indicated on the status line. Pressing [Ins] again switches back to *Insert* mode. In *Insert* mode, you insert a line each time you press [←], and you may insert empty lines by pressing [Ctrl][N].

With these few commands, you can enter and edit your notes. Now let's turn to the function keys on the command line.

[F2] Save

This command saves the contents of your note file on disk. This is never done automatically, and you must therefore **remember to Save** your note file before you shut down the computer. You may also use [Ctrl][K][D] to Save.

[F3] New note file

This command allows you to use a file other than the standard file NOTES. When you press [F3], the message:

New note file:

appears at the status line.

The last file name you used is displayed at first. You can enter another name (the old one will disappear the instant you enter a character), you may edit the current name by backspacing through it, or you may use it as it is by pressing [←]. Or you may press [Ctrl] [U] to cancel the command and return to the current file. You could enter, for example:

MYNOTES.TXT

If you enter a file name, that file will be read into the Notepad if it exists; otherwise you will get a blank file. The file is not actually created on disk until you Save it.

If you have made changes to your current note file which have not been saved, you will be asked if you want to Save that file before overwriting it with the new file.

If you want to use a note file that's on another DOS directory, you can include a *DOS path* in the file name, for example:

C:\TEXT\MYNOTES.TXT

Instead of a normal file name, you may enter a file name *pattern*. A pattern is a file name containing *wildcards*. Now, what are *wildcards*? They are special characters which mean 'anything'. There are two such wildcards; asterisk: *and question mark: ?. An asterisk means that any *series* of characters may be present here, and a question mark means that any *single* character may be present in this position. Let's look at some examples:

.
Means files with any first name and any last name, i.e. all files.

*.TXT
Means all files with any first name and the last name TXT.

??.?
Means all files with two-character first names and one-character last names.

And so on, ad infinitum—we're sure you got the idea. You may set up any pattern, mixing asterisks, question marks, and text. When you enter such a pattern, a window opens containing all file names matching that pattern:

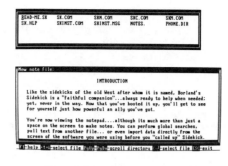

Figure 2-4: File Directory Window

You may now move freely among these file names using the arrow keys, and leaf through multiple-page directories with the [PgUp] and [PgDn] keys (as indicated on the new command line at the bottom of the screen). You select a file by placing the cursor at its name and pressing [◄┘].

You then return to the Notepad, and the new file will be read in. If you don't want to select any file, just press **Esc**, and you return to your old note file. In this way the command may be used just to view the directory of your disk.

[F4] Import data from screen

This is a very exciting feature; it allows you to take text from the screen and put it into the Notepad! When you hit [F4], the Notepad disappears, but don't be afraid, it will come back.

The screen you now see is the one you had before you opened the Notepad window, and the cursor sits at the upper left corner. You may move it around on the screen with the arrow keys, and use the *block marker* commands [Ctrl][K][B] and [Ctrl][K][K] to mark any rectangular block of text. Here's how:

Move the cursor to the beginning of the block you want to import to Notepad, hold down the [Ctrl] key and type [K] and [B] to mark the block **b**eginning (the upper left corner of the rectangular block).

Now use the [→] and [↓] keys to move the cursor to the end of the block, i.e. the lower right corner. You'll see the block being clearly marked on the screen as you move along. Note that [Num Lock] must not be active.

You may press ⌨Ctrl⌨K⌨K⌨, or just ⌨Esc⌨, to end the block and return to the Notepad. Move to the point where you want to insert the block you just marked and press ⌨Ctrl⌨K⌨C⌨ for block copy. Voila—your marked text is moved into the note file.

Imagine how you can use this! You may create reports with the Notepad editor, and then move data right into them from your spreadsheet. Or you may pick out any other bits and pieces of data from **any** other program and put them into your note file. You may then, if you want, include the note file in any large document that you prepare with your normal text editor. We could go on forever, but we are sure this feature will carry your own imagination beyond the horizons.

You can also *paste* **from** the Notepad **to** other programs as explained a little later.

⌨F9⌨ **Expand window**
When you press this key once, the arrow keys will move the borders of the Notepad window outwards, expanding its size. At this point, it is already at its maximum width, but you may also expand it to fill the entire screen in height. When you press ⌨F9⌨ again, the arrows return to their normal use.

⌨F10⌨ **Contract window**
When you press this key once, the arrow keys will move the borders of the Notepad window inwards, contracting its size. When you press ⌨F10⌨ again, the arrows return to their normal use.

⌨Esc⌨ Takes you out of Notepad and back whence you came.

Cut and Paste

Let's say you want to move data from one program to another. It could be part of a spreadsheet that you need to move into a report you are preparing with your word processor.

Sidekick will help you do that. Here's how:

First call up your spreadsheet and **import** the data you need into the Notepad as explained above (⌨F4⌨-import data). This is the 'cutting' part of cut and paste.

Now get ready to 'paste'. Move the cursor to the beginning of the block of numbers you want to paste into your editor and press:

[Ctrl] [K] [B]

to mark the beginning of the block. Then move the cursor to the end of the block you want to paste and press:

[Ctrl] [K] [K]

to mark the end of the block. You will then see the block being marked on the screen.

Once that is done, press:

[Ctrl] [K] [E]

to assign a *paste key.* You are then asked to press a key. Choose a key that you don't use for anything else. Try the:

[Alt] [F10]

key combination (hold down [Alt] and press [F10]).

Now Sidekick will ask you whether you want to paste an entire *block* or whether you want to paste it as separate *lines. Line* will paste the block you have marked one line at a time, and wait for you to press [←┘] after each line. *Block* will paste the entire block without interruption.

Since you are pasting this block into your word processor, you should press

[B]

to choose **b**lock paste. Line paste is useful if you want to paste data the other way, *into* the spreadsheet.

That's it—you are ready to paste. Press:

[Ctrl][Alt]

to leave the Notepad. Then exit the spreadsheet, enter your word processor, and load your report.

Now move to the place in the report where you want the spreadsheet data pasted in and press:

[Alt][F10]

The block that is marked in the Notepad is now pasted into your document.

This feature is described in greater detail on page 54.

This is by no means all there is to be said about the Notepad, but you'll have to read Chapter 3 for the full details. Here, we will go on with the next window: the Calculator.

Let's assume you are still in Notepad. If not, please press [Ctrl][Alt] and [N] to call it up again.

Sidekick - Owner's Handbook

Calculator

You are in the Notepad. Suppose you now need a calculator. You could [Esc]ape your way out of Notepad and open the Calculator window, of course, but there is an easier and better way: just press [Alt][C], and the calculator pops up, with the Notepad remaining on the screen:

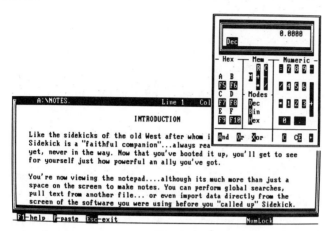

Figure 2-5: Calculator Window

This is why we recommend the use of [Alt] commands to open windows throughout Sidekick: you may use an [Alt] command anywhere in the system to open another window, although it is never shown on the command line. And all [Alt] commands are mnemonics, reminding you of the names of windows:

[H] for **H**elp,
[N] for **N**otepad,
[C] for **C**alculator,
[L] for ca**L**endar,
[D] for **D**ialer,
[A] for **A**SCII table, and
[S] for **S**etup.

Another nice thing about the [Alt] key: if you hold it down for more than about one and a half seconds, Sidekick feels that you need a little help, and up pops the main selection window.

When you activate the Calculator, the *NumLock* status is automatically set, so you may use the numeric keypad to enter numbers without pressing [Num Lock] first.

The *numeric* field in the far right part of the Calculator window (which looks like a calculator's number pad) shows you the keys available for decimal number entry and calculation.

Numbers are entered and calculated exactly as you would do it on a piece of paper. Entries and intermediate results are shown in the display at the top of the window. The final result of a calculation is obtained by pressing [=] or [←].

You may use parentheses to change the order of calculation. For example:

2 * 3 + 4 = **10** [two times three, plus four, equals ten]

whereas:

2 * (3 + 4) = **14** [two times (the result of three plus four), equals fourteen].

Six levels of parentheses are available. Each time you press a [(], it will show up in the display, and each time you press [)], the result of that parenthesis will be calculated and one (will disappear from the display.

Any number on the display may be transferred to your application (or to Notepad) as explained later.

[←]   Deletes digits one at a time, from right to left.

[E] **Clear Entry**
Clears the display, but not previous entries or intermediate results.

[C] **Clear**
Clears the entire Calculator (except memory).

M Memory

Accesses the Calculator's memory. After M, you must press:

C   to clear the memory.
R   to recall the number in memory to the display. The number in memory remains unchanged.
=   to put the number on the display into memory.
+   to add the number on the display to the number in memory.
-   to subtract the number on the display from the number in memory.
*   to multiply the number in memory with the number on the display.
/   to divide the number in memory with the number on the display.

When memory contains a number other than zero, an **M** will be shown in the display.

Modes

The Calculator normally works in *decimal* mode, but if you press B or H, you will switch to *binary* or *hexadecimal* mode. If that baffles you, don't worry, you won't need it. It's something programmers use. Decimal notation is the one we all know, and that is the standard notation of the Calculator. The use of binary and hexadecimal is discussed further in Chapter 4.

Pasting Numbers From the Calculator

You will probably quite often want to use numbers from the Calculator somewhere else—in your spreadsheet, word processor, database, or in Notepad. You do this by 'pasting' the number to a key. When you later press that key, the number comes out.

It's quite simple: press P to invoke **p**aste. Then press the key that you want to paste the number to.

This may be any key, but of course it is practical to choose a key that you don't use for any other purpose, because as long as it holds a number from the Calculator, its normal function is suspended. Use something like Alt P, for example, that reminds you that this is a **p**aste key. Or, if you paste a series of numbers, you could use, for example, Alt 1, Alt 2, etc.

Suppose that you have a number in the Calculator display. Now press `P` for **paste** and then `Alt` `P` to paste the number to that key combination. Then leave the Calculator and return to what you were doing. Press `Alt` `P` again, and the number from the Calculator appears. You can repeat this as many times as you like; the number stays in the key until cleared.

If you want to return the key to its normal use (which removes the number from the key at the same time), that's also easy. Simply return to the Calculator and press **P** again. Now press **C** to clear all keys of any numbers you have pasted to them.

That's all about the Calculator for now; you will find more details in Chapter 4.

Well then, let's go on to the next window: the caLendar. You could press `Esc` to return to Notepad, and open the caLendar window from there. But for now, leave the Calculator on your screen and open the caLendar window from here.

caLendar

Press Alt L , and the caLendar pops up in the upper left corner of the screen. It will initially display April 1985, unless your PC is set to a later date.

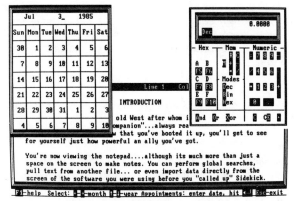

Figure 2-6: caLendar Window

You may now move through time: press ← and → to change months and ↑ and ↓ to change year. The caLendar covers 1901 through 2099.

Let's try something else: leave the caLendar on the screen and press ⏎. You'll see a new window, containing an appointment pad for the day displayed.

You can enter a note about the day on the top line; the following lines are for appointments from 8 a.m. through 8:30 p.m. in half-hour intervals. To enter a note, move to the desired time using the ↓ or ↑ keys and enter your appointment followed by ⏎. The PgUp and PgDn keys switch between page 1 and 2 of each day, and you may use ← and → to change date.

The function keys you see on the bottom line are used as follows:

F2 Name
Press F2 and enter the name or initials of the person whose appointment caLendar you will use. The name must be no more than 8 characters long, and may contain only letters (A through Z) or numbers (0 through 9).

[F3] **Print**

[F3] is used to print one day, or a period of days, from the current appointment caLendar. You are asked to specify the first date and the last date.

You may just press [←] when asked for *first month,* and printing will start from the first appointment in the caLendar. Then enter the last date you want to print. Again you may just press [←], and the printing will continue until the date of the last appointment in the caLendar.

[F4] **Print all**

is used to print all appointments in the current appointment caLendar.

[F5] **Delete**

[F5] is used to delete one day, or a series of days, from the current appointment caLendar. You'll have to specify the first and last date of this period of time. If you just press [←] when asked for *first month,* the deletions will start with the first one found. Then enter the last date you want to delete. If you press [←] once again, all appointments until yesterday's date will be deleted.

Well, that's enough about the caLendar for the present. If you need more information, it's in Chapter 5. For now, let's go on to the next window: the Dialer.

Dialer

The Dialer turns your computer into an automatic telephone dialer provided that you have a modem connected to your computer. It must be a Hayes modem or compatible, an AT&T 4000 modem, or a PCjr modem on the IBM PCjr. The VOAD Keyboard Phone is also supported.

'My communications package does the same thing' you might say. Sure, but does it do it while you are in the middle of your database, word processor, spreadsheet, or BASIC? Or does it pick phone numbers from any other program and dial them for you? Since we know the answers, we know you will use the Sidekick Dialer a lot.

Before using the Dialer, you must tell Sidekick which communications port your modem is on. This is done with the installation program SKINST (see page 101).

As with the other windows, you may activate the Dialer while the caLendar window is open. Instead, we'd like to demonstrate a very nice feature of the Dialer, so please [Esc]ape your way out of Sidekick.

Now fire up your customer database, if you have one, or anything else that displays phone numbers of people you frequently call. It could be as simple as a text file that you maintain with your word processor. Or you can simply type a phone number at the DOS prompt, for example:

123-4567

If you do that, it's a good idea to press [Esc] instead of [←] at the end of the number, because [Esc] will make DOS ignore it, and you won't get an error message from DOS.

Note that the number must contain a hyphen or at least one parenthesis.

Now press [Ctrl][Alt] again to activate Sidekick.

With Sidekick's main selection window on the screen, press [Alt][D] (or [D] or [F5], if you prefer) to activate the Dialer. The first phone number on the screen is pointed out, and you can make the call by pressing [←].

```
ANDX  90(800)-792-9992   Anadex (Printers)
BB    90(609)-426-4254   Byte Books
CP    90(415)-786-0909   CompuPro (S100,CPU,68000)
ERI   90(314) 725-5566   EnerTronics (graphics,3D,software)
INF        90555-1212    Information
PH    90(609)-927-3770   Plum Hall (Unix,C,Books)
```

```
F1-help F2-New file <--dial | -scroll  search: F3-ID F4-all F5-stop Esc-exit
```

Figure 2-7: Dialer Window

Sidekick "knows" a phone number, because it contains special characters. These are usually parentheses or hyphens, but you can choose other characters with the installation program.

To make things very clear: in order to distinguish a phone number from dates, amounts, and other numeric information, the phone number must not contain commas, periods, or slashes.

If you have more than one number on the screen that looks like a phone number, the first one will be chosen. You can then move to the next one by pressing ⊡. If you don't want to dial the number on the screen, but use the Dialer's own phone directory, you just press the space bar.

If the Dialer cannot find a valid phone number on the screen, it will load its own phone directory file if it is present on your disk.

The phone directory file must be a standard text file and may be prepared with the Notepad, with a database program, or with a Pascal or BASIC program you have written. See Chapter 6 for details about this file.

The default name of the phone directory file is **PHONE.DIR**, but you may choose another default name in the Setup window.

Once the file is loaded, it is displayed in the Dialer window, with a horizontal bar pointing at the first entry. You may scroll your file up and down using the arrow keys, and press ⏎ to dial when the desired number is displayed in the bar. Or you may press one of the following keys:

F2 New file
This function key lets you specify a new phone directory file. The default name is PHONE.DIR (unless you have changed the default value in the Setup window), but you can have as many different phone directory files on your disk as you wish, and use F2 to switch between them.

F3 Search INITials
When you want to call a particular person, simply press F3 and enter the person's initials. *Initials* are anything starting in column one of each line in the phone directory—it could be anything you choose. The dialer will then find the number in the directory, and you then press ⏎ to dial it.

F4 Search all
You press F4 to search the *entire directory* for any text (as opposed to *search INIT* which only searches for text starting in column one). This way you can search for addresses, professions, or any other information you have put into the file.

F5 Stop search
Stops a search and returns the ↓ and ↑ keys to their normal scroll functions.

Using the Dialer Without a Modem

If you don't have a modem connected to your computer, you can still use the Dialer. It won't dial numbers for you, of course, but you can use it as a 'Rolodex' file to keep track of your phone numbers.

Done with the Dialer, we shall proceed to the ASCII table. If you don't know what ASCII is, and if you couldn't care less, then skip the next section—you won't miss it. It's something programmers will love, though.

ASCII table

Press ⌐Alt ⌐A⌐ to open the ASCII table. This window shows the entire 256-character ASCII character set, 16 or 32 characters at a time. Use the arrows to leaf through the pages.

The first two pages show 16 ASCII values at a time, in decimal and hexadecimal; they show the characters as they look on the PC's screen, and they tell you the control character value and mnemonic of each character.

The remaining pages display 32 characters at a time, with values in decimal and hexadecimal, and the characters as they are displayed on the screen.

Let us suppose that you are in BASIC, and you want to draw a nice frame on the screen. You'll use a series of:

PRINT CHR$(.)

statements.

But what values should you use to produce vertical and horizontal lines, corners, etc.?

To find out, activate Sidekick, open the ASCII table, and leaf through it until you find the symbols you need. In this case they are in the last part of the table, so you should start by leafing backwards using ⌐←⌐ or ⌐↑⌐. The values you need are displayed right next to their symbols.

And remember: ⌐→⌐ and ⌐↓⌐ move you forwards through the ASCII table. The ⌐←⌐ and ⌐↑⌐ move backwards.

This is not only easier than finding them in a book; the symbols on the screen also make it much easier to choose the right one. This is because this is the *exact* symbol that your program will produce on the screen—not a near-look-alike as you will find in a printed table.

That's it, folks. You can now use Sidekick to your heart's content.

The Setup window is not covered here, as its use is entirely optional. It is used to change some of Sidekick's standard values, and save the changes, so that they become new standard values; you may, for example, save the current size and positions of your windows. But as long as you are satisfied with Sidekick as it is, you need not use the Setup window. Chapter 8 covers Setup in detail.

The next section shows you how to use the Sidekick windows in a slightly more advanced way; you may read it now if you feel ready for it, or you may come back later.

Advanced Use

This section will show you how to speed up your use of Sidekick.
Once you are familiar with the general way of opening and closing
Sidekick windows, you will want to use these techniques.

Returning to an Open Window

As you have learned, you may open a window either by selecting
from the main selection window, or by entering an [Alt]-command
from any window that is already open. And you close a window by
[Esc]aping out of it.

Now suppose that you started with Notepad, then opened the
Calculator window, and finally opened the ASCII table:

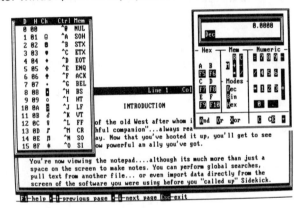

Figure 2-8: Notepad - Calculator - ASCII table

... and now you want to get back to the Notepad. You may press [Esc]
twice, of course, closing the ASCII table and Calculator windows
behind you. But you might need these windows on-screen when
you return to the Notepad—perhaps for reference, or because you
want to import data from them to the Notepad.

Instead of [Esc]aping back to the Notepad, you therefore press [Alt][N]
to go straight back to it. The Notepad is now restored, but the
Calculator and ASCII windows remain on the screen, partly
obscured by the Notepad:

```
 D  H Ch  Ctrl Mem
 0 00      ^@  NUL                                    ┌─────────────────────────┐
 1 01  ☺   ^A  SOH                                    │                  0.0000  │
 2 02  ☻   ^B  STX                                    │  Dec                     │
 3 03  ♥   ^C  ETX                                    └─────────────────────────┘
 4 04  ♦   ^D  EOT                              ─ Hex ─┬─ Mem ─┬─ Numeric ─
 5 05  ♣   ^E  ENQ                                     │   R C │  ▪ 7 8 9 ▪
 6 06  ♠   ^F  ACK                              A  B   ⌐ + ⌐   │
 7 07  •   ^G  BEL                              F5 F6  │ * ⌐   │  ▪ 4 5 6 ▪
                                                C  D   ┴ Modes
 A:\NOTES.              Line 2   Col 7   Insert        Indent
┌──────────────────────────────────────────────────────────────────────┐
│              ─                INTRODUCTION                              │
│                                                                        │
│  Like the sidekicks of the old West after whom it is named, Borland's  │
│  Sidekick is a "faithful companion"...always ready to help when needed;│
│  yet, never in the way. Now that you've booted it up, you'll get to see│
│  for yourself just how powerful an ally you've got.                    │
│                                                                        │
│  You're now viewing the notepad....although its much more than just a  │
│  space on the screen to make notes. You can perform global searches,   │
│  pull text from another file... or even import data directly from the  │
│  screen of the software you were using before you "called up" Sidekick.│
└──────────────────────────────────────────────────────────────────────┘
 F1─help F2─save F3─new file F4─import data F9─expand F10─contract Esc─exit
```

Figure 2-9: Back to the Notepad

If you press ⎡F4⎤ to import data, the Notepad disappears, and the Calculator and ASCII table become fully visible.

What has happened is that while the original sequence of open windows was:

1:Notepad - 2:Calculator - 3:ASCII table

it has been changed to:

1:Calculator - 2:ASCII table - 3:Notepad

This means that when you now ⎡Esc⎤ape from the Notepad, you return to the ASCII table, then ⎡Esc⎤ape from the ASCII table to Calculator, and finally ⎡Esc⎤ape out of Sidekick.

Whenever you return directly to a window that is already open, Sidekick automatically performs this 'reshuffling' of the windows.

Getting Out—And Quickly Back In

Let's assume you have a number of Sidekick windows open; you are in the middle of some complicated work. Now you need to return to your application for a while, but you would like to return to exactly the same setup of Sidekick's windows, without having to open them all again.

Just press [Ctrl][Alt], and you return to the world outside Sidekick. You may now do whatever you need to do out there, and when you press [Ctrl][Alt] again to get back into Sidekick, you return to the exact same window setup that you left.

[Ctrl][Alt] (or both [⇧] keys), used *from within Sidekick*, immediately returns you to the outside world, and the next time you press them, you are returned to where you left off in Sidekick.

Time and Date Stamping Notes

The Notepad has a special feature which automatically time and date stamps orders, notes on telephone conversations, or anything else that you need logged with time and date.

Simply enter the text:

.LOG

in column one, line one of your note file. Whenever you open the Notepad window with such a file loaded, the cursor moves to the bottom of the file, and the time and date from the PC's clock is written there.

A time and date stamp may also be written with the [Ctrl][Q][T] command which reads the current time and date from the PC's clock into the file, or with the [Ctrl][Q][O] command which mimics a .LOG file by jumping to the end of the file and **then** inserting the time and date.

This short ride with your Sidekick should have given you a good idea of what it can do for you. The following chapters describe each Sidekick window in detail and are useful for reference whenever you want to know more.

Chapter 3
NOTEPAD

The Notepad is a full-screen text editor providing all the facilities of the *TURBO Pascal* editor, and many of those of *WordStar.* If you are familiar with either of these editors, you need but little instruction in the use of the Notepad. There are a few minor differences, and the Notepad has a few extensions; these are discussed on pages 63 and 66 . You should also read page 40 which deals with the function keys available in Notepad.

Using the Notepad is simple as can be: press Alt N to open the Notepad window, and the Notepad appears:

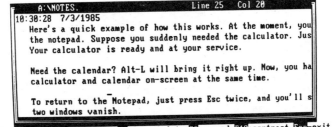

```
     A:\NOTES.                        Line 25   Col 20
 10:30:28  7/3/1985
       Here's a quick example of how this works. At the moment, you
       the notepad. Suppose you suddenly needed the calculator. Jus
       Your calculator is ready and at your service.

       Need the calendar? Alt-L will bring it right up. Now, you ha
       calculator and calendar on-screen at the same time.

       To return to the Notepad, just press Esc twice, and you'll s
       two windows vanish.

   F1-help F2-save F3-new file F4-import data F9-expand F10-contract Esc-exit
```

Figure 3-1: Notepad Window

You type text on the keyboard, just as if you were using a typewriter. To terminate a line, you may press the ⏎, or you may let Sidekick's automatic word wrap take care of things. When you exceed the right margin while typing a word, a line break will be inserted, and that word will be moved to the next line.

When you have typed enough lines to fill the window, the top line will scroll up and out of the window. But don't worry, it is not lost. You may page back and forth through your text using the editing commands described a little further on.

Let us first take a look at the meaning of the *command line* at the bottom of the screen.

The Notepad Command Line

The bottom line of the screen shows you which function keys you may use, and what they do. Let's look at them more closely:

⟨F1⟩ Help

The Help key will display detailed help about Notepad, provided that the Help file SK.HLP is on the disk drive and directory from which you first started Sidekick.

⟨F2⟩ Save

Save the contents of your note file on disk. The old file is unchanged, and is given the last name **BAK**. You may also use the WordStar command ⟨Ctrl⟩⟨K⟩⟨D⟩ to Save.

In order to let you change disks while using Sidekick, files are never saved automatically, and you must therefore remember to Save before you shut down the computer.

⟨F3⟩ New note file

This command allows you to use a file other than the standard file NOTES. When you press ⟨F3⟩, the message:

New note file:

appears on the status line. The last name you specified is displayed initially. You can enter another name (the old one will disappear the instant you enter a character), you may edit the current name by backspacing through it, or you may use it as it is by pressing ⟨⏎⟩. Or you may press ⟨Ctrl⟩⟨U⟩ to cancel the command and return to the current file.

If you enter a file name, that file will be read into the Notepad if it exists. Otherwise you will get a blank file. The file is not actually created on disk until you Save it.

If you have made changes to your current note file which have not been saved, you will be asked if you want to Save that file before the new file is read in.

Instead of a normal file name, you may enter a file name *pattern*. A pattern is a file name containing *wildcards*. Now, what are *wildcards*? They are special characters which mean 'anything'. There are two such wildcards; asterisk: * and question mark: ?. An asterisk means that any *series* of characters may be present here, and a question mark means that any *single* character may be present in this position. Let's look at some examples:

.

Means files with any first name and any last name, i.e. all files.

*.TXT

Means all files with any first name and the last name TXT.

??.?

Means all files with two-character first names and one-character last names.

And so on, ad infinitum. You may set up any pattern, mixing asterisks, question marks, and text. When you enter such a pattern, a window containing all file names matching that pattern will open.

A file may be chosen from this directory by moving to the desired file name and pressing ⏎. The PgDn and PgUp keys are used to leaf through multiple-page directories. Esc returns you to Notepad, and no new file will be selected.

Notepad normally looks for its files on the directory you are currently using, unless you have chosen a different default directory in Setup (see Chapter 8). You can work on files in other directories by specifying a path name in front of the file name in the standard DOS format. For instance:

`\text\letters\myletter`

specifies the file MYLETTER in the directory LETTERS which is a sub-directory to TEXT, which is a sub-directory to the root directory.

F4 Import data from screen

This is a very exciting feature; it allows you to take text from the screen and put it into the Notepad! When you press F4 , the Notepad disappears. But don't worry—it will be back.

The screen you now see is the one you had before you opened the Notepad window, with the cursor sitting at the upper left corner. You may move it around on the screen with the cursor control keys, and use the *block marker* commands `Ctrl` `K` `B` and `Ctrl` `K` `K` to mark any rectangular block of text. This is how:

Move the cursor to the upper left corner of the block you want to import to Notepad, hold down the `Ctrl` key and press `K` and `B` to mark the block **beginning**. Now use the `→` and `↓` keys to move the cursor to the the lower right corner of the block. You'll see the block being marked on the screen as the cursor moves along.

You may mark the end of the block with `Ctrl` `K` `K`, but it is not necessary. You can just press `Esc`, and you return to the Notepad. Move to the point where you want to insert the block you just marked and press **Ctrl-K-C** for block **c**opy.

You can also *paste* a block from the Notepad to other programs; see page 54 for details.

`F9` **Expand window**
Pressed once, this key causes the arrow keys to move the borders of the Notepad window outwards, expanding its size, until they reach the edge of the screen. The maximum Notepad size is 23 lines by 78 characters. When pressed again, `F9` returns the arrows to their normal use.

`F10` **Contract window**
Pressed once, this key causes the arrow keys to move the borders of the Notepad window inwards, contracting its size, until the minimum Notepad size of 3 lines by 40 characters is reached. When pressed again, `F10` returns the arrows to their normal use.

`Esc` Takes you out of Notepad and back whence you came.

The Status Line

The top line of the window is the *status line*. It gives you the following information:

```
path X:FILENAME.TYP Line n Col n Insert Indent Graph
```

Figure 3-2: Notepad Status Line

path X:FILENAME.TYP
The directory, drive, name, and type of the file being edited. Some types, indicated by *file extensions* like .EXE, .COM, and .BAT mean something to DOS, so don't use these. Other types have meaning only to people; things like .TXT for a text file, .HLP for a help file, or maybe .TIM for a Notepad you use to keep track of your time.

Please refer to your DOS documentation for a full explanation of file names and paths.

Line n
Shows the number of the line containing the cursor, counted from the start of the file.

Col n
Shows the number of the column containing the cursor, counted from the left side of the Notepad.

Insert
Indicates that characters typed on the keyboard will be inserted at the cursor position. Existing text to the right of the cursor will move to the right as you write new text. Pressing [Ins] or [Ctrl][V] will instead activate the **Overwrite** mode. Text typed on the keyboard will then type over any characters already there.

Indent
Indicates that auto-indentation is on. Switch off/on with [Ctrl][Q][I].

Graph
Graph is toggled on and off by pressing [Ctrl][Q][G]. When **on**, the Notepad will display the PC's semi-graphic character set. When **off**, which it is by default, these characters will be shown as normal characters. This allows you to edit WordStar document files.

Editing Commands

As mentioned before, you write text in the Notepad as if you were using a typewriter. As this is a computerized text editor, however, it offers you a number of editing facilities which make text manipulation much easier than on paper.

The Notepad accepts a total of 51 commands to move the cursor around, page through the text, find and replace text strings, etc., etc. These commands can be grouped into the following four categories:

Cursor movement commands
Insert and delete commands
Block commands
Miscellaneous commands

Each of these groups contain logically related commands which will be described separately in following sections. To make things clear in your mind, please go over the following table, which provides an overview of the commands available:

CURSOR MOVEMENT COMMANDS:

Character left	To top of window
Character right	To bottom of window
Word left	To top of file
Word right	To end of file
Line up	To end of file with
Line down	time/date stamp
Scroll up	To left on line
Scroll down	To right on line
Page up	To beginning of block
Page down	To end of block
	To last cursor position

INSERT & DELETE COMMANDS:

Insert mode on/off	Delete right word
Insert line	Delete character under cursor
Delete line	Delete left character
	Delete to end of line

BLOCK COMMANDS:	MISC. EDITING COMMANDS:
Mark block begin	End edit
Mark block end	End tab
Mark single word	Auto indent off/on
Copy block	Restore line
Move block	Set right margin
Delete block	Re-format paragraph
Read block from disk	Find
Write block to disk	Find & replace
Hide/display block	Repeat last find
Print block	Control character prefix
Sort block	Time/date stamp
Paste block	Graphics on/off

Table 3-1: Editing Command Overview

In a case like this, the best way of learning is by doing. So open the Notepad window, specify a file (or use the standard file NOTES), and try out the commands as you read on.

Each of the following descriptions consists of a heading defining the command, followed by the default keystrokes used to activate the command. In some cases, there are two ways of giving a command: either the PC's function keys (arrows and such), or the *WordStar* commands; both will be shown.

If you are used to a different editor, you may re-define any commands to suit your taste. How to do that is described on page 97. The following descriptions of the commands assume the use of the *WordStar*-compatible keystrokes.

A Note on Control Characters

All commands are issued using control characters. A control character is a special character generated by your keyboard when you hold down the [Ctrl] key (right next to the [A] on your keyboard) and press any key from A through Z (well, even the [, \,], ^, and _ keys generate control characters, for that matter).

The ⎡Ctrl⎤ key works like the ⎡⇧⎤ keys: if you hold down ⎡⇧⎤ and press ⎡A⎤, you will get a capital A; if you hold down ⎡Ctrl⎤ and press ⎡A⎤, you will get a Control-A (⎡Ctrl⎤⎡A⎤).

Cursor Movement Commands

The most basic thing to learn about the Notepad is how to move the cursor around in the window. The Notepad uses a special group of control characters to do that, namely the control characters ⎡A⎤, ⎡S⎤, ⎡D⎤, ⎡F⎤, ⎡E⎤, ⎡R⎤, ⎡X⎤, and ⎡C⎤.

Why these? Because they are conveniently located close to the ⎡Ctrl⎤ key, so that your left little finger can rest on that while you use the middle and index fingers to activate the commands. Furthermore, the characters are arranged in such a way on the keyboard as to logically indicate their use. Let's examine the basic movements: cursor up, down, left, and right:

These four characters are placed so that it is logical to assume that ⎡Ctrl⎤⎡E⎤ moves the cursor up, ⎡Ctrl⎤⎡X⎤ down, ⎡Ctrl⎤⎡S⎤ to the left, and ⎡Ctrl⎤⎡D⎤ to the right. And that is exactly what they do.

Try to move the cursor around in the window with these four commands. As the PC keyboard has repeating keys, you may just hold down the ⎡Ctrl⎤ key and one of these four keys, and the cursor will move rapidly across the window.

Now let us look at some extensions of those movements:

The location of ⎡Ctrl⎤⎡R⎤ next to ⎡Ctrl⎤⎡E⎤ implies that ⎡Ctrl⎤⎡R⎤ moves the cursor up, and so it does, but a whole page at a time. Similarly, ⎡Ctrl⎤⎡C⎤ moves the cursor down one page at a time.

It's the same way with ⌈Ctrl⌉⌈A⌉ and ⌈Ctrl⌉⌈F⌉: ⌈Ctrl⌉⌈A⌉ moves to the left like ⌈Ctrl⌉⌈S⌉, but a whole word at a time, and ⌈Ctrl⌉⌈F⌉ moves one word to the right.

The two last basic movement commands do not move the cursor but scroll the entire window upward or downward in the file:

⌈Ctrl⌉⌈W⌉ scrolls upward in the file (the lines in the window move down), and ⌈Ctrl⌉⌈Z⌉ scrolls downward in the file (the lines in the window move up).

Character left   ⌈←⌉ or ⌈Ctrl⌉⌈S⌉
Moves the cursor one character to the left without affecting the character there. This command does not work across line breaks: when the cursor reaches the left edge of the window, it stops.

Character right   ⌈→⌉ or ⌈Ctrl⌉⌈D⌉
Moves the cursor one character to the right without affecting the character there. This command does not work across line breaks: when the cursor reaches the right edge of the window, the text starts scrolling horizontally until the cursor reaches the extreme right of the line, in column 250, where it stops.

Word left   ⌈Ctrl⌉⌈←⌉ or ⌈Ctrl⌉⌈A⌉
Moves the cursor to the beginning of the word to the left. A word is defined as a sequence of characters delimited by one of the following characters: space <>, ; . ( ) []^' *+- /$. This command works across line breaks.

Word right   ⌈Ctrl⌉⌈→⌉ or ⌈Ctrl⌉⌈F⌉
Moves the cursor to the beginning of the word to the right. See the definition of a word above. This command works across line breaks.

Line up   ⌈↑⌉ or ⌈Ctrl⌉⌈E⌉
Moves the cursor to the line above. If the cursor is on the top line, the window scrolls down one line.

Line down `↓` or `Ctrl` `X`

Moves the cursor to the line below. If the cursor is on the second-last line, the window scrolls up one line.

Scroll up `Ctrl` `W`

Scrolls 'up' towards the beginning of the file, one line at a time (the entire window scrolls down). The cursor remains on its line until it reaches the bottom of the window.

Scroll down `Ctrl` `Z`

Scrolls 'down' towards the end of the file, one line at a time (the entire window scrolls up). The cursor remains on its line until it reaches the top of the window.

Page up `PgUp` or `Ctrl` `R`

Moves the cursor one page up with an overlap of one line. The cursor moves one window less one line backward in the text.

Page down `PgDn` or `Ctrl` `C`

Moves the cursor one page down with an overlap of one line. The cursor moves one window less one line forward in the text.

The commands discussed so far let you move freely around in your Notepad text, and they are easy to learn and understand. Try to use them all for a while and see how natural they feel.

Once you master them, you may want to move more rapidly. The Notepad provides commands to move rapidly to the extreme ends of lines, to the beginning and end of the text, and to the last cursor position.

These commands require **two** characters to be entered: first a `Ctrl` `Q` and then one of the following control characters: `S`, `D`, `E`, `X`, `R`, or `C`. They repeat the pattern from before:

`Ctrl` `Q` `S` moves the cursor to the extreme left of the line, and `Ctrl` `Q` `D` moves it to the extreme right of the line.

`Ctrl` `Q` `E` moves the cursor to the top of the window, `Ctrl` `Q` `X` moves it to the bottom of the window.

`Ctrl` `Q` `R` moves the cursor all the way 'up' to the start of the file, `Ctrl` `Q` `C` moves it all the way 'down' to the end of the file.

To left on line   `Home` or `Ctrl` `Q` `S`
Moves the cursor all the way to the left edge of the window (column one).

To right on line   `End` or `Ctrl` `Q` `D`
Moves the cursor to the end of the line, in other words, to the position following the last printable character on the line. Trailing blanks are always removed from all lines to preserve space.

To top of window   `Ctrl` `Home` or `Ctrl` `Q` `E`
Moves the cursor to the top of the Notepad window.

To bottom of window   `Ctrl` `End` or `Ctrl` `Q` `X`
Moves the cursor to the bottom of the Notepad window.

To top of file   `Ctrl` `PgUp` or `Ctrl` `Q` `R`
Moves to the first character of the text.

To end of file   `Ctrl` `PgDn` or `Ctrl` `Q` `C`
Moves to the last character of the text.

Finally, the `Ctrl` `Q` prefix with a `B`, `K`, `0`, or `P` command allows you to jump far within the file:

To beginning of block   `Ctrl` `Q` `B`
Moves the cursor to the position of the *block begin* marker set with `Ctrl` `K` `B` (hence the B). The command works even if the block is not displayed (see *hide/display block* later), or the *block end* marker is not set.

To end of block   `Ctrl` `Q` `K`
Moves the cursor to the position of the *block end* marker set with `Ctrl` `K` `K` (hence the K). The command works even if the block is not displayed (see *hide/display block* later), or the *block begin* marker is not set.

Go to End-of-file and stamp with time/date   `Ctrl` `Q` `O`
This command places the cursor at the end of the file and reads the time and date from the PC's clock and writes it into the file.

To last cursor position   `Ctrl` `Q` `P`
Moves to the last position of the cursor (the **P** being a mnemonic for Position). This command is particularly useful to move back to the last position after a **S**ave operation or after a find or find/replace operation.

Insert and Delete Commands

These commands let you insert and delete characters, words, and lines. They can be divided into three groups: one command which controls the text entry mode (insert or overwrite), a number of simple commands, and one extended command.

Notice that the Notepad provides a 'regret' facility which lets you 'undo' changes *as long as you have not left the line*. This command (`Ctrl` `Q` `L`) is described on page 58.

Insert mode on/off   `Ins` or `Ctrl` `V`
With this command you switch between insert and overwrite modes while entering text. The current mode is displayed in the status line at the top of the window.

Insert mode is the default value when the Notepad is activated, and it lets you insert new text into an existing text. The existing text to the right of the cursor simply moves to the right while you type in the new text.

Overwrite mode may be chosen if you wish to replace old text with new text. In this mode, characters are replaced by the new characters typed over them.

Delete left character ⬅

This is the 'back space' key right above the ⬅ key—not to be confused with ⊡ on the numeric block. It moves one character to the left and deletes the character there. Any characters to the right of the cursor move to the left.

Delete character under cursor [Del] or [Ctrl][G]

Deletes the character under the cursor and moves any characters to the right of the cursor one position to the left. This command does not work across line breaks.

Delete right word [Ctrl][T]

Deletes the word to the right of the cursor. A word is defined as a sequence of characters delimited by one of the following characters: space <>, ; . ( ) []^' *+- /$. This command works across line breaks, and may thus be used to remove line breaks.

Insert line [Ctrl][N]

Inserts a line break at the cursor position. The cursor does not move.

Delete line [Ctrl][Y]

Deletes the line containing the cursor and moves any lines below one line up. The cursor moves to the left edge of the window. **No provision exists to restore a deleted line, so be careful!**

Delete to end of line [Ctrl][Q][Y]

Deletes all text from the cursor position to the end of the line.

A **block** of text is deleted with the *delete block* command [Ctrl][K][Y] described in the next section.

Block Commands

All block commands are extended commands; they each require two keystrokes.

You may ignore them for now if you feel a bit dazzled at this point. Later on, when you feel the need to move, delete, or copy large chunks of text, you should return to this section.

A block of text is simply any amount of text, from a single character to several pages. A block is marked by placing a *Begin block* marker at the first character and an *End block* marker at the last character of the desired portion of the text. Thus marked, the block may be copied, moved, deleted, or written to a file.

A command is available to read an external file into the text as a block, and a special command conveniently marks a single word as a block.

Mark block begin   F7 or Ctrl K B

This command marks the beginning of a block. The marker itself is not visible on the screen, and the block only becomes visibly marked when the *End block* marker is set.

You may also use the *Begin block* marker as a reference point in your text, and jump directly to it with the Ctrl Q B command.

Mark block end   F8 or Ctrl K K

This command marks the end of a block. As above, the marker itself is not visible on the screen, and the block only becomes visibly marked when the *Begin block* marker is also set.

You may also use the *End block* marker as a reference point in your text, and jump directly to it with the Ctrl Q K command.

Mark single word   Ctrl K T

This command marks a single word as a block, supplementing the *Begin block - End block* sequence which is a bit clumsy when marking just one word.

If the cursor is placed within a word, then this word will be marked; if not then the word to the left of the cursor will be marked. A word is defined as a sequence of characters delimited by one of the following characters: space <>, ; . ( ) []^' *+- /$.

Hide/display block   `Ctrl` `K` `H`

This command causes the visual marking of a block to be toggled off
and on. Block manipulation commands (copy, move, delete, or write
to a file) work only when the block is displayed. Block-related cursor
movements (jump to beginning/end of block) work whether the
block is hidden or displayed.

Copy block   `Ctrl` `K` `C`

This command places a copy of a marked and displayed block
starting at the cursor position. The original block is left unchanged,
and the markers are placed around the new copy of the block.

This command is also used to move data from the screen into the
Notepad, together with the `F4` function key (import data).

Move block   `Ctrl` `K` `V`

This command moves a marked and displayed block from its
original position to the cursor position. The block disappears from
its original position and the markers remain around the block at its
new position.

Delete block   `Ctrl` `K` `Y`

This command deletes a marked and displayed block. **No provision
exists to restore a deleted block, so be careful!**

Read block from disk   `Ctrl` `K` `R`

This command is used to read a file into the current text at the cursor
position, exactly as if it were block that was moved or copied. The
file read in is marked as a block.

When you use this command, you are prompted for the name of the
file to read. The file specified may be any legal file name. If you just
press ⏎, or specify a file *pattern*, you get a directory matching the
pattern from which you can choose your file.

Write block to disk [Ctrl] [K] [W]

This command is used to write a previously marked block to a file. The block is left unchanged, and the markers remain in place. When you use this command, you are prompted for the name of the file to write to. If the file specified already exists, a warning is given before the existing file is overwritten.

If no block is marked, nothing will happen. The file specified may be any legal file name. Avoid the use of files of the type .BAK, as it is used for Notepad backup files.

Print block [Ctrl] [K] [P]

This command is used to print the marked (and displayed) block on the printer. If no block is marked, or if a marked block is hidden, the entire file is printed.

Sort block [Ctrl] [K] [S]

This command sorts lines within a marked and displayed block. You are asked to specify the first and last column of the **key** on which the sort is performed. The columns you used last are displayed initially. You can enter other values (the old ones will disappear the instant you enter a number), you may edit the current values by backspacing through them, or you may leave them unchanged.

Paste block [Ctrl] [K] [E]

This is Sidekick's 'cut-and-paste' feature. A block marked in the editor may be assigned to almost any key on the keyboard. When that key is pressed, the marked block is transmitted, just as if you were typing it at the keyboard.

The [Ctrl] [K] [E] command defines the key you want paste with. You may use any of the [F1] through [F10] function keys **alone** or **in combination** with [⇧], [Ctrl], or [Alt].

The rest of the keyboard can also be used as paste keys, but **only** in combination with [Alt]. Consequently, you **cannot** paste with, for example, the [A] or the [9] key, but you **can** use the [Alt] [A] or the [Alt] [9] key combinations.

A key **combination** is achieved by holding down [⇧], [Ctrl], or [Alt] while pressing the desired key. To produce [Ctrl] [F8], for example, you hold down the [Ctrl] key while you press [F8].

When you have defined the key you want to use for paste, you are asked if you want to paste by **B**lock or by **L**ine.

Block paste means that the entire marked block will be played back when you press the paste key, exactly as if it had been typed at the keyboard, only much faster. This method is useful for pasting text into a word processor, for example.

Line paste means that each time you press the paste key, **one line** of the marked block is played back. No ⏎ (RETURN) is sent. This is useful for pasting data into a spreadsheet.

When you mark a block for **Line** paste, you should place the block end marker **at the end** of the last line. If you place the end marker at the beginning of the following line, you will get a blank line at the end of the pasted block.

The marked lines are played back cyclically. This means that if you have marked three lines, the first line will be played back the first time you press the paste key. The second and third depressions will play back lines two and three. The fourth time you press the paste key, the **first** line will be played back again, and so forth.

The key (or key combination) you have defined now becomes the **paste key**. Whenever you mark a block in the Notepad, the block will be assigned to that key and played back when the key is pressed.

The normal use of the paste key is suspended while the block is marked or until the paste is removed by pressing Ctrl K E Del .

The text pasted to a key is determined by the positions of the block markers. The key is in effect as long as the block is marked and not hidden. If the block markers are moved to another position, a new block will be pasted to the key.

If the block is deleted (Ctrl K Y) or hidden (Ctrl K H), nothing is pasted to the key, which then has its usual effect. The paste is not deleted, however. A subsequently marked block will be assigned to the same key.

You can only have one paste key in effect at a time. If you assign another, any existing pastes will be deleted.

If you want to transfer data from the screen outside the Notepad to another application ('cut and paste'), you must first **import** the data from the screen into the Notepad (press [F4]); then mark it as a block, and finally paste it.

Blocks and lines are normally transmitted to the receiving program at full speed, which is close to 1000 characters per second. Some programs may have difficulty receiving input at that speed; they will start beeping furiously at you, or you may lose characters. If that happens, you may increase the *Paste delay factor* in the Setup window to slow down transmission.

Remove paste   [Ctrl] [K] [E] [Del]
This command removes the pasted text from the paste key and returns it to its normal use, whether or not a block is marked in the Notepad.

Miscellaneous Editing Commands

This section collects a number of commands which don't seem to belong to any of the above categories. They are nonetheless important.

Save file   [F2] or [Ctrl] [K] [D]
Saves the note file and gives the original file (if any) the last name **.BAK**.

Tab   [⇤] or [Ctrl] [I]
There are no fixed tab positions in the Notepad. Instead, tab positions are automatically set to the beginning of each word on the line just above the cursor.

This is especially useful when making notes or an outline, because you often want to line up columns of related items.

Auto indent off/on ⌈Ctrl⌉⌈Q⌉⌈I⌉

The auto indent feature provides automatic line indentation. When active, the indentation of the current line is repeated on each following line.

In other words, when you press ⌈◄┘⌉, the cursor does not return to column one, but to the starting column of the line you just terminated.

When you want to change the indentation, use any of the cursor right or left commands to select the new column. When auto indent is active, the message **Indent** is displayed on the status line. When passive, the message is removed. Auto indent is active by default.

Graphics on/off ⌈Ctrl⌉⌈Q⌉⌈G⌉

The **Ctrl-Q-G** command toggles Notepad's graphics mode on and off. When graphics is on, the word **Graph** is displayed on the status line.

As graphics is OFF by default, the editor normally displays only the first 128 ASCII characters, so you can't see most of the semi-graphics and foreign characters. This allows you to display text files produced by editors which use the 8th bit of the characters (like WordStar).

When you switch graphics ON, you can see all 256 ASCII characters. To enter a character from the the extended character set, you would hold down the ⌈Alt⌉ key and enter the character's decimal ASCII value **on the numeric keypad**. You have 1.5 seconds to do that before Sidekick's Main Selection Window pops up.

Note that on the IBM AT and on the PC and XT with a keyboard enhancer such as *SuperKey,* you must press ⌈⇧⌉⌈Alt⌉ to enter extended characters.

You can use Sidekick's ASCII table to find these values; please check page 33.

Restore line   Ctrl Q L

This 'OOPS!' command lets you regret changes made to a line **as
long as you have not left the line**. The line is simply restored to its
original contents regardless of what changes you have made. But
only as long as you remain on the line; the second you leave it,
changes are there to stay. For this reason, the *Delete line* (Ctrl Y)
command can regrettably only be regretted, not restored.

Set right margin   Ctrl O R

The editor supports automatic *word wrap*. This means that when
you reach the right margin during typing, a line break will be
inserted, and the last word will be moved to the next line if it doesn't
fit within the margins.

The *Set right margin* command lets you set the right margin. When
you press Ctrl O R, you will see the current margin. You can enter
another value (the old one will disappear the instant you enter a
number), you may edit the current value by backspacing through it,
or you may press ⏎ to leave it unchanged. This value is saved
permanently in Sidekick when you *Save window setup* (press Alt S
to get the Setup window).

You can disable word wrap by setting the right margin to column
250.

Reformat paragraph   Ctrl B

This command reformats an entire paragraph of text to fit within the
current margins. Reformatting takes place from the cursor position
to the end of the paragraph. A paragraph ends when the next line is
either blank or it contains one or more leading spaces.

If you want to reformat a larger piece of text consisting of many
paragraphs, you must repeat the command for each paragraph.

Find   Ctrl Q F

The Find command lets you search for any string of up to 30
characters. When you use this command, the status line is cleared,
and you are prompted for a search string.

The search string you used last is displayed at first. You can enter
another string (the old one will disappear the instant you enter a
character); you may edit the current string with the Character Left,
Character Right, Word Left, and Word Right commands; or you may
press ⏎ to use it as it is.

The search string may contain any characters, including control characters. Control characters are entered into the search string with the [Ctrl] [P] prefix: enter, for example, a [Ctrl] [A] by holding down the [Ctrl] key while pressing first [P], then [A].

If you want to find a line break, you should search for a [Ctrl] [M] [Ctrl] [J] sequence.

Another handy tool you can use here is [Ctrl] [A]. [Ctrl] [A] has a special meaning: it matches any single character and may be used as a wild card in search strings. You use it by pressing [Ctrl] [Q] [F] (to tell Sidekick you want to search for something) and then typing in part of your search string. When you come to the part of your search string that can be 'anything', press [Ctrl] [P] and then [Ctrl] [A].

When the search string is specified, you are asked for search options. The options you used last are displayed at first. You can enter other options (the old ones will disappear the instant you enter a character), you may edit the current options by backspacing through them, or you may press [←] to use them again.

Terminate the list of options (if any) with [←], and the search starts. If the text contains a target matching the search string, the cursor is positioned at the end of the target. The search operation may be repeated by the *Repeat last find* command ([Ctrl] [L]).

The following options are available:

B   Search backwards, from the current cursor position towards the *beginning* of the text.

n   n =any number. Find the n'th occurrence of the search string, counted from the current cursor position.

U   Ignore upper/lower case. Regard upper and lower case alphabeticals as equal.

W   Search for whole words only. Skip matching patterns which are embedded in other words.

Examples:

W   Search for whole words only. The search string 'term' will only match the word 'term', not the word 'terminal'.

BU   Search backwards and ignore upper/lower case. 'Block' will match both 'blockhead' and 'BLOCKADE', etc.

125 Find the 125th occurrence of the search string.

Find and Replace   `Ctrl` `Q` `A`

The Find and Replace command lets you search for any string of up to 30 characters and replace it with any other string of up to 30 characters.

As you enter this command, the status line is cleared, and you are prompted for the search string. The search string you used last is displayed at first. You can enter another string (the old one will disappear the instant you enter a character), you may edit the current string with the *Character Left, Character Right, Word Left,* and *Word Right* commands; or you may press ⏎ to use it as it is.

The search string may contain any characters, including control characters. Control characters are entered into the search string with the `Ctrl` `P` prefix. For example, enter a `Ctrl` `A` by holding down the `Ctrl` key while pressing first `P`, then `A`.

As with `Ctrl` `Q` `F`, a `Ctrl` `A` has a special meaning in search strings: it can be used as a 'wildcard' because it matches any character.

When the search string is specified, you are asked to enter the string to replace the search string. The replacement string you used last is displayed at first and you can re-use it, edit it, or enter another string of up to 30 characters.

You enter and edit control characters as described above, but `Ctrl` `A` has no special meaning in the replace string. If you just press ⏎ the target will be replaced with nothing. In other words, it will be deleted.

If you want to include a line break in your replacement string, you should enter a `Ctrl` `M` `Ctrl` `J` sequence.

Finally, you are prompted for options. The options you used last are displayed at first and you can re-use them, edit them, or specify new options. The search and replace options are:

B   Search and replace backwards, from the current cursor position towards the *beginning* of the text.

G   Global search and replace. Search and replace in the entire text, irrespective of the current cursor position.

n   *n* =any number. Find and replace *n* occurrences of the search string, counted from the current cursor position.

N   Replace without asking. Do not stop and ask *Replace (Y/N)* for each occurrence of the search string.

U   Ignore upper/lower case. Regard upper and lower case alphabeticals as equal.

W   Search and replace whole words only. Skip matching patterns which are embedded in other words.

Examples:

N10 Find the next ten occurrences of the search string and replace without asking.

GWU Find and replace whole words in the entire text. Ignore upper/lower case.

Terminate the list of options (if any) with ⏎, and the search and replace operation starts.

You can speed up the process by pressing *any* key now. The screen will then no longer show each replacement as it occurs. This is especially useful if you have specified a GN (global, no-asking) option. Note that the key you press will actually be entered into the Notepad, so it is a good idea to use a key that does not print anything—a ↓, for example.

Depending on the options specified, the string may be found. If it is found (and the **N** option is not specified), the cursor is positioned at the end of the target, and you are asked the question:

```
Replace (Y/N)?
```

on the prompt line at the top of the window. Press Y to replace or N to skip. You can also abort the search and replace operation at this point with the Abort command (Ctrl U).

The search and replace operation may be repeated by the *Repeat last find* command (Ctrl L).

Repeat last find   Ctrl L
This command repeats the latest *Find* or *Find and Replace* operation exactly as if all information had been re-entered.

Control character prefix   Ctrl P
The Notepad allows you to enter control characters into the file by prefixing the desired control character with Ctrl P . Control characters are shown as highlighted capital letters.

This is a handy feature, because control characters may be used to vary your printer's output, to produce condensed printing, etc. For example: if you want to enter a Ctrl O to cause the Epson printer to print condensed, hold down the Ctrl key while you press P , and then O . Consult your printer's manual if you need more information about which command does what with your printer. If you are writing *Display macros* for SuperKey (the keyboard enhancer available from Borland International), you will use the Ctrl P prefix to enter Ctrl B 's and Ctrl D 's into the text to control colors or intensities.

Time/date stamp   Ctrl Q T
This command reads the time and date from the PC's clock and then writes it into the Notepad at your cursor's position. The time is written on the military's 24-hour format as *Hours:Minutes:Seconds*. The date is displayed in the American *Month/Day/Year* format.

Abort operation   Ctrl U
The **Ctrl-U** command lets you abort any command in process whenever it pauses for input, like when Search and Replace asks *Replace Y/N?*, or during entry of a search string or a file name (block Read and Write).

Notepad vs. WordStar

If you know *WordStar,* you will notice that a few Notepad commands work slightly differently, and although Notepad naturally contains but a subset of *WordStar's* commands, we have included some commands not found in *WordStar.* We'll look at these differences in this section.

WordStar Text Files

WordStar files written in **D**ocument mode contain a lot of characters with the 8th bit set high (that is, characters with ASCII values between 128 and 255). In non-graphics mode, Notepad ignores the 8th bit and displays normal characters.

WordStar files may also contain lines which are not terminated by the standard CR/LF (Carriage Return /Line Feed) sequence. Instead they are terminated with a lone CR or LF (you'll see a '-' or a 'J' in the right margin in WordStar). Since Sidekick's Notepad will insert the missing character in such lines, you'll have to be careful not to save such a file from Notepad if you will later use it with WordStar.

Graphics

In graphics mode (press [Ctrl][Q][G]), Notepad can display the PC's foreign and semi-graphic characters. This means that WordStar files containing characters with a high 8th bit will look very odd indeed on the screen. Use non-graphics mode for such files.

Cursor Movement

The cursor movement controls [Ctrl][S], [Ctrl][D], [Ctrl][E], and [Ctrl][X] (or [←], [→], [↑], and [↓]) move freely around in the window and do not jump to column one on empty lines. This does not mean that the window is full of blanks; on the contrary, all trailing blanks are automatically deleted.

[Ctrl][S] and [Ctrl][D] do not work across line breaks. To move from one line to another, use [Ctrl][E], [Ctrl][X], [Ctrl][A], [Ctrl][F], or [Del].

Word Wrap and Page Breaks

WordStar has two different kinds of line breaks: the 'hard' ones produced by pressing ⏎, and the 'soft' ones produced by the automatic word wrap.

Notepad's automatic word wrap produces 'hard' line breaks. 'Soft' line breaks are not used by Notepad, but it will recognize WordStar's soft line breaks.

Only the right margin can be set in Notepad; the left margin is always column one.

Notepad will not display WordStar's page breaks, nor will it produce page breaks of its own.

Page breaks may be inserted manually with Ctrl P Ctrl L . This inserts an ASCII form feed directly into the text

Dot Commands

Notepad will not recognize any WordStar dot commands, but introduces its own .LOG directive for automatic time and date stamping.

Mark Single Word

Ctrl K T is used to mark a single word as a block which is more convenient than the two-step process of marking the beginning and the end of the word separately.

End Edit

The Ctrl K D command does save the file on disk, but it leaves you inside Notepad. The F2 function key does the same. To exit from the Notepad, press Esc.

Line Restore

The Ctrl Q L command restores a line to its contents before edit *as long as the cursor has not left the line.*

Tabulator
> No fixed tab settings exist. Instead, tabs are automatically set to the start of each word on the line immediately above the cursor.

Auto Indent
> The ⌈Ctrl⌉⌈Q⌉⌈I⌉ command switches the auto indent feature on and off.

Time and Date Stamping Notes
> A file with the directive:

> `.LOG`

> entered in column one of line one is a *LOG file*. Whenever the Notepad window is opened with such a file active, the cursor moves to the bottom of the file, and the time and date from the PC's clock is written there. The cursor then jumps to the next line.

> The commands ⌈Ctrl⌉⌈Q⌉⌈T⌉ and ⌈Ctrl⌉⌈Q⌉⌈O⌉ also read time and date and put them into the file.

Print Block
> The **Ctrl-K-P** command is used to print a marked and displayed block on the printer. If no block is displayed, the entire file is printed.

Sort Block
> The ⌈Ctrl⌉⌈K⌉⌈S⌉ command causes lines within a marked and displayed block to be sorted.

Paste Block
> The ⌈Ctrl⌉⌈K⌉⌈E⌉ command is used to paste a marked block to a key. When you press this key, the marked block is transmitted, as if it were entered from the keyboard.

Notepad vs. the TURBO Pascal Editor

Notepad is almost identical to the TURBO Pascal editor, but it has some extensions as described in the following sections.

Graphics

In graphic mode (press `Ctrl` `Q` `G`), Notepad can display the PC's foreign and semi-graphic characters.

Time and Date Stamping Notes

A file with the directive:

    .LOG

entered in column one of line one is a *LOG file*. Whenever the Notepad window is opened with such a file active, the cursor moves to the bottom of the file, and the time and date from the PC's clock is written there. The cursor then jumps to the next line.

The commands `Ctrl` `Q` `T` and `Ctrl` `Q` `O` also read time and date and put them into the file.

Word Wrap and Paragraph Re-format

The Notepad has automatic word wrap. When a word cannot fit within the right margin as set by the `Ctrl` `O` `R` command, the word is moved down to the next line automatically.

`Ctrl` `B` is used to reformat paragraphs, one paragraph at a time.

Print Block

The **Ctrl-K-P** command is used to print a marked and displayed block on the printer. If no block is displayed, the entire file is printed.

Sort Block

The `Ctrl` `K` `S` command causes lines within a marked and displayed block to be sorted.

Paste Block

The `Ctrl` `K` `E` command is used to paste a marked block to a key. When this key is pressed, the marked block is transmitted, as if it were entered from the keyboard.

Notes:

Chapter 4
CALCULATOR

The Sidekick Calculator resembles a handheld calculator and performs the four basic arithmetic operations, using BCD (Binary Coded Decimal) arithmetic for highest possible accuracy. It displays 18 digits with 4 decimal positions, and thus has a range of -99,999,999,999,999.9999 through 99,999,999,999,999.9999.

The memory functions let you perform calculations directly on the contents of the Calculator's memory.

The Calculator operates in decimal, hexadecimal, and binary modes and performs conversion between them.

When the Calculator is activated, the *NumLock* status is automatically set, which enables the use of the numeric keypad. NumLock is returned to its previous state when you leave the Calculator.

The **numeric** field in the right part of the window shows you the keys available for decimal entry and calculation. You enter numbers for calculation according to normal algebraic rules. Parentheses may be used to change the order of calculation. For each level of parentheses entered, one left parenthesis will appear in the display. When a closing parenthesis is entered, one level of parentheses will be closed, the expression will be calculated and displayed, and one parenthesis will disappear from the display. Any number on the display may be transferred to your application (or to Notepad) as explained later.

⬅ Deletes digits one at a time, from right to left. This is the key on the top row, next to **NumLock**, not the left arrow key on the numeric keypad.

E **Clear Entry**
    Clears the display, but not previous entries or intermediate results.

C **Clear**
    Clears the entire Calculator (except memory).

[M] Memory

Accesses the Calculator's memory. After [M], you must press:

[C]   to clear the memory.
[R]   to recall the number in memory to the display. The number in memory remains unchanged.
[=]   to put the number on the display into memory.
[+]   to add the number on the display to the number in memory.
[−]   to subtract the number on the display from the number in memory.
[*]   to multiply the number in memory with the number on the display.
[/]   to divide the number in memory with the number on the display.

When memory contains a number other than zero, an **M** will be shown in the display.

Modes

The Calculator operates in decimal mode by default, but pressing [B] or [H] will switch to binary or hexadecimal mode and convert the number on the display and in memory accordingly. The function keys [F5] through [F10] are used to enter the hexadecimal digits A through F.

The binary range is 20 digits: 0 through 11111111111111111111, and the hexadecimal range is 12 digits: 0 through FFFFFFFFFFFF.

The [A], [O], and [X] keys perform the logical operations **And, Or,** and **Xor.**

Pasting Numbers From the Calculator

The Calculator lets you 'paste' a number from the display into any other application. Press [P] to invoke *Paste*. Then press the key that you want to use for the paste operation.

This may be any key, but it is practical to choose a key that is not used for other purposes, because as long as it holds a number from the Calculator, its normal function is suspended. Use, for example, a function key or a letter or number in combination with [Alt] or [Ctrl].

You may paste numbers to as many keys as you wish, and use them anywhere you want, perhaps to store intermediate results that you may need later in a calculation. In this way, you can add as many 'memories' as you want to your calculator.

To clear the keys, and return them to their normal use, you press [C] while in 'programming mode'. This clears all keys of numbers that you have pasted to them.

Notes:

Chapter 5
CALENDAR

When activated, the caLendar will initially display April 1985, unless the date in PC-DOS is set to a later date. The caLendar covers 1901 through 2099.

Today's date is highlighted. Use ⬅ and ➡ to move from month to month or ⬆ and ⬇ to move from year to year.

To open the appointment caLendar, press ⏎ to open today's appointments, or enter a date and press ⏎. The appointment caLendar's window then opens, displaying an appointment schedule for that date.

The top line is for a note on the day, and the following lines are used to enter appointments in half-hour intervals from 8 a.m. through 8:30 p.m. The ⬇ and ⬆ keys are used to position the cursor on the desired time. The PgDn and PgUp keys switch between page 1 and 2 of each day, and the ⬅ and ➡ keys change the date. The function keys shown on the bottom line are used as follows:

F2 Name

Press F2 and enter the name or initials of the person whose appointment caLendar you will use. The name must be no more than 8 characters, and may contain only letters from A through Z or numbers.

The appointment caLendar keeps a separate file for each person. The first name of this file is the person's name or initials, and the last name is normally APP, but you may change this in Setup (Chapter 8). Appointment files are placed in the root directory unless another directory is specified in Setup.

F3 Print

F3 is used to print one day or a part of the current appointment caLendar. You are asked to specify the first date and the last date. If you just press ⏎ when asked for *first month*, printing will start from the first appointment in the caLendar. Then enter the last date you want to print. Again you may just press ⏎, and the date of the last appointment in the caLendar will be chosen.

When printing appointments from the caLendar, Sidekick makes a form feed after each day. If you would like more than one day per page, you can set your printer's PAGE LENGTH to a whole fraction shorter than a full page.

For instance: if you use standard 8 1/2 by 11 inch paper, which is normally 66 lines long, you could set the printer's page length to 33 lines. That way you will get two days per page (22 lines will get you 3 days per page). A full day will require 28 lines, but if you never have that many appointments in a day, you may use a smaller page length.

Please consult your printer's manual or your in-house systems specialist for information on how to set the printer's page length.

F4 Print all
F4 is used to print all appointments in the current appointment caLendar.

F5 Delete
F5 is used to delete one day or a period of time from the current appointment caLendar. The first and last date of this period must be specified. If you just press ⏎ when asked for *first month*, you will delete from the first appointment in the caLendar. Then enter the last date you want to delete. Again you may just press ⏎, and yesterday's date will be chosen. All appointments in the specified period are then deleted.

Chapter 6
DIALER

The Dialer comes pre-installed for a Hayes Smartmodem (300, 1200, or 1200B), or compatible modem. Another modem may be chosen in the installation procedure.

The Dialer works in two different ways:

1) It may pick a phone number off the screen. This facility may be used to dial numbers found by other programs.

2) It may use its own telephone directory file. If the Dialer cannot find a valid phone number on the screen when you activate it, it will load the directory file instead, if it is present.

How does the Dialer find a phone number on the screen? It must contain certain *required* characters. These are: hyphens and parentheses. If a number contains one or more of either, it will be recognized as a phone number—provided that it doesn't contain periods, slashes, or other characters which are used in dates, amounts, and other numeric information.

The required characters may be changed by the installation program.

If you have more than one number on the screen that looks like a phone number, the first one will be chosen. You can then move to the next one by pressing ⊡. If you don't want to dial the number, but use the Dialer's own phone directory, you just press the space bar.

You can compile your telephone directory in many ways; the easiest is simply to use the Notepad to write it. The contents of each line in the telephone directory should be:

`INITIALS PHONENUMBER COMMENT`

The *INITIALS* may actually be a person's initials, or it may be any other abbreviation or nickname by which you choose to remember your friends, family, or business associates. The identifier is unique only because it starts in column one (leading blanks are significant).

The *PHONENUMBER* must contain one of the special characters defined in the installation process. If you use the standard setup, at least one parenthesis or one hyphen must be present.

A **T** in the number will cause the modem to use tone dialing, and a **P** will cause it to use pulse-dialing. Tone-dialing is used if nothing is specified, and the two dialing methods may be mixed within one number, if desired. An @ in the number causes dialing to pause —this is useful for dialing long distance numbers.

COMMENT can be the full name, the address, or a list of keywords which you associate with each person in the directory. For your vendors you could, for example, write a list of the goods or services each provides.

In fact, you can create a small database, and you can use the Notepad's sorting capabilities to organize your phone directories. The dialer displays 78 characters on each line. Your file may have longer lines, but anything beyond the 78th character is ignored.

The following lines are examples of valid entries in the phone directory file:

```
BOR (408) 438-8400 Borland International, Scotts Valley
Borl,408 438-8400,(Sidekick and TURBO Pascal)
Fred 1(888) 623-1234 Computer Cleaners Inc.
```

The Notepad may be used to maintain this file, or it may be a data file created by your database program or by a Pascal or BASIC program you write yourself. Fields in the data file may be either comma-delimited or positional; records must be delimited by a CR/LF sequence.

Once the file is loaded, it is displayed in the Dialer window, with a horizontal bar pointing out the first entry. You may scroll your file up and down using the arrow keys, and press ⏎ to dial when the desired number is displayed in the bar. Or you may press one of the following keys:

F2 New file

This function key lets you specify a new phone directory file. The default name is PHONE.DIR (unless you have changed the default value in the Setup window), but you can have as many different phone directory files on your disk as you wish, and use F2 to switch between them.

F3 search INITials

When you want to call a particular person, you just need to press F3 and enter the person's initials. 'Initials' are anything starting in column one of the phone directory file. The dialer will then find the number in the directory, and you press ⏎ to dial it.

While a search is active, the ↓ and ↑ keys will continue the search for the next match in the indicated direction.

F4 search all

You press F4 to search the *entire line* for any text (as opposed to *search INIT* which only searches for text starting in column one). This way you can quickly locate all vendors offering, for example, COMPUTERS or FAST FOOD, or customers interested in THIS or THAT. The possibilities are countless.

While a search is active, the ↓ and ↑ keys will continue the search for the next match in the indicated direction.

F5 stop search

F5 stops a search and returns the ↓ and ↑ keys to their normal scroll functions.

Chapter 6 - DIALER   **77**

Notes:

Chapter 7
ASCII TABLE

The ASCII table displays the entire 256-character extended ASCII character set, 16 or 32 characters at a time. ASCII is the *American Standard Code for Information Interchange*.

The arrows keys are used to leaf through the pages.

The first two pages show 16 ASCII values at a time, in decimal and hexadecimal; they show the characters as they look on the PC's screen, and they contain the control character value and mnemonic of each character.

The remaining pages display 32 characters at a time, with values in decimal and hexadecimal, and the characters as they look on the screen.

The real value of the ASCII table, apart from the fact that it never gets lost, is that it displays the character set right on the screen, which of course is better than any approximation you may find in a table printed in a book.

Notes:

Chapter 8
SETUP

The *Setup* window is used to change the standard values assumed by Sidekick with regard to file names, directories, positions and size of windows, etc.

Press [Alt] [S] to open the Setup window:

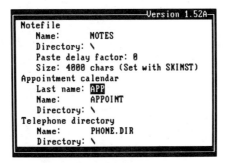

Figure 8-1: Setup Window

You can then use the [↓] and [↑] keys to move the bar to the item you want to change. If you regret a change, press either arrow key, and the old value will come back. When you are sure of a change, press [↵]. This will record the new value and move the bar to the next item.

The following sections describe each item in turn.

Note File

Name

The default note file name is NOTES. You may enter any other legal file name you wish Notepad to use as standard each time you start Sidekick. If the name you specify here is a *pattern* containing *wildcards* (asterisks and question marks), a list of files matching the pattern will be shown when you enter the Notepad, and you can choose a file from that list.

For example, if you specify the name *.TXT,* you will get a list of all files with the last name TXT, and you may select a file from that list.

Directory

Sidekick will use the directory you specify here when it reads and writes its note files—unless you include a path name in the file name when you specify a *New note file* in the Notepad.

Now, what is all this about directories and paths? Well, here's a brief description—for complete details, please see your DOS documentation.

DOS lets you divide your disk space into a *tree-structured directory.* This means that you can collect related files in separate file directories, and you can make a structure of directories that reflects the way you use your files.

Here's a simple example:

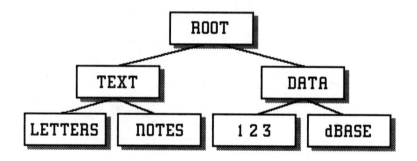

Figure 8-2: Tree-structured File Directory

The directory starts with a *root.* DOS uses a backslash: \ to identify the root. The root has two *sub-directories*: *TEXT* and *DATA.* Each of these has two sub-directories.

You would store your files in these sub-directories. In *LETTERS* you would store your letters, and *NOTES* would be where you keep your Sidekick note files. In *123* you would have Lotus 1-2-3 spreadsheet files, and in *dBASE* you would place your dBASE-III data files.

In this way you can have a large number of files on the same disk, and still have them separated from one another.

DOS uses a *path* to describe the directory *NOTES*:

\TEXT\NOTES

This means: start from the root, go through the directory *TEXT* to the directory *NOTES*.

So, if you wanted to tell *Setup* that you want your note files kept in this directory, you would enter:

\TEXT\NOTES ⏎

By default, no directory is specified. That makes Sidekick place the note file on whichever directory is currently active.

Paste delay factor

This is a number between 0 and 99 which controls the speed with which characters are sent to other programs when *pasting* blocks or lines from the Notepad.

The factor is set to **0** by default; that means **no delay**, i.e. characters are sent at full speed (close to 1000 per second). Some programs may have difficulty handling input at that speed; in that case you can slow down transmission by introducing a 'delay factor' of between **1** and **99**. The actual effect of a particular delay factor may vary depending on which program you paste to, but in any case, the higher the delay factor, the slower the transmission speed.

Size

The default maximum size of the note file is 4000 characters. This size may be changed by the installation program SKINST (see Appendix B).

Appointment caLendar

Last name

The default last name of the appointment caLendar files is .APP. You may enter any other legal last name (0 through 3 characters) that you wish to use as last names of the appointment caLendar files.

If the name you specify here is a *pattern* containing *wildcards* (asterisks and question marks), a list of files matching the pattern will be shown when you enter the Notepad, and you can choose a file from that list. For example, if you enter:

AP? ⏎

you will get a list of all files with three-letter last names starting with AP.

Name

The default first name of the appointment file is APPOINT. You may enter any other legal file name you wish the appointment caLendar to use as standard. Again, you can include *wildcards* in the name to form a pattern.

For example, if you let the last name be APP, and enter an asterisk for the first name, you may choose an appointment file from a list of all files with the last name APP when you first enter the appointment caLendar.

The F2 **Name** command in the appointment caLendar may be used to choose a file with a different first name while you are working with your appointments. The name you specify becomes the first name of the file.

Directory

The default directory is the root directory (indicated with a back-slash as in DOS). This means that the appointment caLendar will expect to find its file in the root directory. You may specify another directory in the standard DOS format.

Please see the explanation of DOS directories on page 82.

Dialer

Name

The default telephone directory file name is PHONE.DIR. You may enter any other legal file name you wish the Dialer to use. If the name you specify here is a *pattern* containing *wildcards* (asterisks and question marks), a list of files matching the pattern will be shown when you enter the Dialer, and you can choose a file from that list.

For example, if you enter:

DIR?.PHO ⏎

the dialer will present you with a list of all files with four letters or less in their first names starting with DIR and the last name PHO. For example:

DIR1.PHO
DIR2.PHO
DIR.PHO

but not:

DIR22.PHO
DIR1.TXT

This is very handy for keeping business and family directories separate.

Directory

The default directory is the root directory (indicated with a backslash as in DOS). This means that the Dialer will expect to find its file in the root directory. You may specify another directory in the standard DOS format.

Please see the explanation of DOS directories on page 82.

Save Setup

When you *Save* your setup, please make sure that the .COM file you used to start Sidekick is in the drive and directory from where you started Sidekick.

This is necessary because Sidekick saves the Setup directly in this file. Please see page 9 for details.

F2 Save file setup

When you press the F2 key, the names, directories and delay factor displayed in the Setup window are saved in Sidekick and become the new standard values.

F3 Save window setup

When you press the F3 key, the current window positions, the current size of the Notepad window, and the Notepad's right margin are saved in Sidekick and become the new standard values.

F4 Save both

When you press the F4 key, both file setup and window setup are saved in Sidekick and become the new standard values.

Appendix A
APPLICATION NOTES

Using an AUTOEXEC.BAT File

Starting Sidekick may be as simple as writing **SK** ⏎ on the DOS command line. But if you are using an AUTOEXEC.BAT file to start up your system, you might as well include Sidekick in it.

If you do that, Sidekick should be the very **last** thing you let AUTOEXEC activate before an application program. Let us take a look at an AUTOEXEC file as it could look if you want to load and run an accounting package—let's call it ACCOUNTS—each time you start the computer:

```
spool
ramdisk
network
clock
accounts
```

Spool, *Ramdisk*, and *Network* are examples of utilities that are loaded into RAM and stay there until the computer is reset, just like Sidekick. As explained on page 11, it is important that Sidekick is the **last** resident program loaded into memory.

So, to include Sidekick in this AUTOEXEC.BAT file, load it into the Notepad and insert sk between clock and accounts:

```
spool
ramdisk
network
clock
sk
accounts
```

Then save the file (press F2), and next time you start your computer, Sidekick will be loaded automatically at the right time.

If you use the tree-structured directories of DOS 2.0 and later, please make sure that you change to the directory where you keep Sidekick and its help file before you start Sidekick. AUTOEXEC.BAT may look like this, for example:

```
chdir \system
spool
ramdisk
network
clock
chdir \sk
sk
chdir \accnt
accounts
```

If you set up a DOS *path* with the command:

```
SET PATH=C:\SYSTEM;C:\SK;C:\ACCNT ⏎
```

you can actually start all the programs from the root. DOS will use the path to find the programs in their directories. **Don't** do that. You **must** be on the directory that contains Sidekick's .COM and .HLP files when you start it, or you cannot save setups or use the help system.

A Few Ideas

Many of the uses of Sidekick are obvious; like using the automatic dialer, making a quick note of something, letting Sidekick keep track of your appointments, or help you convert between decimal and hexadecimal numbers.

Nevertheless, the following might give you some inspiration on how to combine one or more features of Sidekick with your job, your life and some of the programs you usually use.

So, here are some scenes from the real world with and without Sidekick as they could happen to a secretary, a salesperson, a president, a programmer or anyone else using a computer.

Scenes From Our Lives

Scene One:
You are working with a word processor, like WordStar, and you need to make a few calculations in connection with the text you are writing. You do not want the calculations included in the text, only the results. On the other hand you want to keep the calculations for future reference.

Without Sidekick:
First dig out your calculator. Now do the calculations. Now find a piece of paper and a pencil, or write the the numbers with WordStar, then mark the text as a block and write it to a file. When you later on need the notes and calculations for your own reference you must either read in the file as a block, read it and then delete it, or try to find the piece of paper.

With Sidekick:
Activate the Calculator. Do the calculations. Activate the Notepad and write your notes. Press [Esc] twice to return to your word processor.

When you need the notes later on, simply activate the Notepad from within your word processor, read the note and press [Esc] to return to your word processor.

Scene Two:
Something very strange just happened to the program you are running. Unfortunately, the in-house specialist is out to lunch and you know she will not believe you unless you show it to her. On the other hand you can't stop working. What do you do?

Without Sidekick:
1) Continue working and learn to live with the problem; nobody will fix it, because nobody will believe you. Or 2) Stop working and get in trouble with your boss.

With Sidekick:
Activate the Notepad and press [F4] to import data from the screen. Now use the block commands to copy the entire screen to the note file which you may show the in-house specialist later on.

Scene Three:
You are working at your computer when the telephone rings. Someone asks you to call back in two days and leaves a number for you to call.

Without Sidekick
First find your appointment calendar. Then find a pencil and sharpen it (somebody broke its point). Then make a note of the name and telephone number. When the day arrives, you have to find your appointment book again and, for the second time, duplicate the number, this time by pushing buttons on the phone.

With Sidekick:
Activate Sidekick. Select the caLendar and the day to call back. Type the name and telephone number of the person to call back. Press `Esc` to return to your program.

When the day arrives, you simply activate the caLendar as you normally do to check the day's appointments. Since today's the day, and now's the time, press `Alt` `D` to activate the Dialer—it automatically picks the number from the caLendar, and you just press `↵` to dial.

Scenes From the Life of a Salesperson

Scene One:
You are using dBASE III or some other program to keep track of customers. You also use this program to select the customers you need to call.

Without Sidekick:
Although you have an autodial modem in your computer, and although your computer already 'knows' the number you need to dial, it can't, because the database program cannot make phone calls! So what happens? You must read the number off the screen and dial it yourself.

With Sidekick:
Activate Sidekick, then press `Alt` `D` to dial. Sidekick automatically picks the number off the screen and dials it for you.

Scene Two:

Your job requires you to keep a log of your telephone conversations - with whom, on which subject, for how long?

Without Sidekick:

You need to have the following things handy: 1. a block of paper, 2. a pencil (and a sharpener), 3. a telephone directory, 4. a stopwatch. Now you must find the number of the customer to call (unless the customer called you), dial the number, make a note of the current time and date in your log book, make a note of what you talked about and finally note the time again.

With Sidekick:

Activate the Notepad. Each time you pick up the phone, press Ctrl Q T, and the date and time will be entered into the file. Then make your notes about the conversation. Finally, when you hang up, press Ctrl Q T again. Or use a 'log' file to keep track of time for you (see page 66).

Use Sidekick's Dialer to dial the number.

Scenes From the Life of a Programmer

Scene One:

For some reason you need the binary representation of an ASCII character.

Without Sidekick:

You **know** that you left your ASCII table right next your keyboard only 10 seconds ago, but somehow it has managed to disappear into another dimension. Finally you find a book with an ASCII table, but unfortunately it contains only the decimal values. Well, thank Texas Instruments for your programmer's calculator - if only Bob hadn't borrowed it and run down the batteries.

With Sidekick:

Press Alt A for ASCII-table and find the character. Press Alt C to activate the Calculator. Enter the decimal value and tell the Calculator to convert to binary.

A Few Ideas.

Scene Two:
You are writing a large BASIC program with lots of GOTOs and GOSUBs. But you keep forgetting the line number of your input routine, or the meaning of line numbers such as 8760.

Without Sidekick:
You very quickly end up with endless lists of notes on paper—which you must keep updated all the time. (And you end up with some unbelievable spaghetti code you'll have to maintain later.)

With Sidekick:
Use the Notepad to maintain lists of your subroutines. Notepad's *search* command lets you quickly locate any subroutine in the list, and the *sort* command lets you keep the list sorted—on line numbers, on names, or on anything else.

You might choose to avoid this problem altogether by using Borland's TURBO Pascal which lets you assign meaningful names to procedures such as: *GetEntry, UpdateFile, GetCustomerName*, etc. TURBO Pascal gets rid of spaghetti code and puts all the fun back in programming—and it's so fast you won't believe it!

Scene Three:
You are repeatedly assembling, running, and editing an assembly language program.

Without Sidekick:
If the assembler produces any error messages, you must stop the output and copy the error messages from the screen. Then you start your editor and, based on your notes, you find the error and correct it.

With Sidekick:
Simply let the assembler produce output to a file. When you go back to work on the assembly code, use Notepad as a window into the file with the error messages.

Appendix B
INSTALLATION

The installation program SKINST can be used to change the default values of:

- Screen type
- Notepad commands
- Notepad file size
- Notepad right margin
- Dialer
- Colors
- Sidekick activate command ('hot key').

Type:

SKINST ⏎

to start the installation program. One or more of the Sidekick program files:

SK.COM, SKN.COM, SKC.COM, and *SKM.COM*

must be on the logged drive. Only the Sidekick *files* will be installed; not the Sidekick possibly residing in memory during installation. The changes made by the installation program become effective only when Sidekick is restarted.

```
            Installation program for SideKick 1.50

          Choose installation item from the following:

  Screen type | notepad Commands | Notepad size | right Margin

    Dialer     | cOlors          | Activate commands

            Enter S, C, N, M, D, O, A or Q to quit:_
```

Figure B-1: Installation Main Menu

Choose the item you want to install from this menu by pressing one of the highlighted capital letters.

These are the things you should know about your computer when you install Sidekick:

Which monitor adapter(s) are installed?
Monochrome Monitor Adapter or equivalent (Hercules, for example), Color Monitor Adapter, both Monitor Adapters.

Which asynchronous communications port does your modem use?
COM1
COM2

Screen Type

When you press ⑤ to perform screen installation, you get this menu which lets you select the display you want Sidekick to use:

```
Choose one of the following displays:

0)  Default display mode
1)  Monochrome display   (includes Hercules card)
2)  Color display 80x25
3)  B/W   display 80x25  (one-color monitor connected to color graphics card)

Which display? (0-3 or ◄┘ for no change): 0_
```

Figure B-2: Screen Installation Menu

The various screen choices are described in the following. Notice that Sidekick always uses *80x25 character mode.*

Default display

Sidekick will pop up on the display that's currently active. This is the way Sidekick is set up by default, and the way you should use it unless you have a special reason to want Sidekick to pop up on one particular display.

Note that you should always install for *Default display* if you have a multi-display adapter, for example, the *Paradise Multidisplay Card*, even if you have multiple screens attached to it.

If you have two monitors attached to *two separate video adapters* you can make Sidekick pop up on one particular monitor, regardless of which monitor is active. You do that by installing Sidekick for one of the following displays:

Monochrome display

Sidekick will pop up on the monochrome display, no matter which display is active, and switch back to the display that was previously active when you exit Sidekick.

Monochrome display refers to the high-resolution, text-only display connected to a monochrome display controller and should not be confused with the *black and white* display which refers to a single-color monitor connected to a color graphics adapter.

Monochrome also includes *Hercules* and compatible boards, for example *AST Preview* and *AST Monograph Plus*.

Color display 80x25

Sidekick will pop up on the color display, no matter which display is active, and switch back to the display that was previously active when you exit Sidekick.

This mode assumes a color monitor connected to a color graphics adapter.

B/W display 80x25

Sidekick will pop up on the black and white display, no matter which display is active, and switch back to the display that was previously active when you exit Sidekick.

This mode assumes a single-color monitor connected to a color graphics adapter, and Sidekick will use only shades of gray. It should not be confused with the *monochrome* display.

A Note On Graphic Displays

Sidekick always uses the screen's *text mode*. If you are displaying graphics on the screen when you activate Sidekick, it will turn into scattered blots of strange characters in different colors, and Sidekick will appear on top of this. Not to worry. When you exit Sidekick, your graphics will return. Do not import data when the display is in graphics mode.

The Hercules and compatible adapters present special problems, since they handle graphics differently from the IBM standard. Sidekick does its best to determine the type of hardware in your computer and handle it properly.

Some boards which claim to be Hercules compatible, however, may not be 100% so, and Sidekick may be fooled into believing it's another type of adapter. We do try to make Sidekick work with as many types of display adapters as possible, but if yours is not truly compatible, you may have problems when you activate Sidekick while displaying graphics.

Blinking Display?

If you install default, color, or b/w displays, you are finally asked if your screen blinks when it scrolls. A standard IBM color/graphics adapter blinks, but many other adapters don't. Answer Y or N as appropriate. This causes Sidekick to use your video controller optimally, with as little screen 'noise' as possible.

Notepad Commands

The Notepad responds to a number of commands which are used to move the cursor around on the screen, delete, insert and move text, etc.

Each of these functions may be activated by either of two commands: a primary command or a secondary command. The secondary commands are installed by Borland and comply with the 'standard' *WordStar* set, and they cannot be changed. Some primary commands have been installed to let you use the function keys, arrows, etc. on the PC's keyboard, but you may use the installation program to change them or install other primary commands. Only the primary commands are displayed by the installation program.

When you press C for Command installation, the first command appears:

CURSOR MOVEMENTS:

1: Character left   <ESC> K ->

This means that the character sequence [Esc][K] (produced by the ←️ key) has been installed to move the cursor one character left. If you want to change this command, you may enter the desired command following the -> prompt in either of two ways:

1) Press the key you want to use. It could be a function key or any other key or sequence of keys (max. 4). The installation program responds with a mnemonic of each character it receives. If you want to use [F5] to perform 'Insert line', just press [F5] followed by ⏎ when you reach *Insert line* in the installation sequence:

22: Insert line   Nothing -> <ESC> ?

‹ESC› ? represents F5 (like in TURBO Pascal), and F5 is now installed as the primary command to insert a line. The secondary command Ctrl N will remain in effect as long as no primary command is installed as Ctrl N.

2) Instead of pressing the actual key you want to use, you may enter the ASCII value(s) of the character(s) in the command. The values of multiple characters are entered separated by spaces. Hexadecimal values are entered with a dollar-sign in front of them, like: $1B.

In both cases, terminate your input by pressing ⏎. Note that the two methods—pressing the command key directly, or entering the command's ASCII value—cannot be mixed within one command. In other words: if you have started defining a command sequence by pressing keys, you must define all characters in that command by pressing keys and vice versa.

You may press - to remove a command from the list, or B to back through the list one item at a time.

The Notepad accepts a total of 51 commands, and they may all be installed. If you make an error in the installation, for instance, if you define the same command for two different purposes, you will get a self-explanatory error message, and you must correct the error before terminating the installation. A primary command, however, may conflict with one of the WordStar-like secondary commands; that will just render the secondary command inaccessible.

This is a list of all secondary (WordStar) commands and those primary commands that we installed for you (and the keys you press to use them). There's space for you to note your own commands here. Hint: Use a pencil—you *will* change your mind somewhere along the way.

ACTION	SECONDARY COMMAND	PRIMARY COMMAND	PC KEY

CURSOR MOVEMENTS:

1: Character left	`Ctrl` `S`	<ESC> K `←`	
2: Alternative	`Ctrl` `H`	_ _ _ _ _ _	
3: Character right	`Ctrl` `D`	<ESC> M `→`	
4: Word left	`Ctrl` `A`	<ESC> s	`Ctrl` `←`
5: Word right	`Ctrl` `F`	<ESC> t	`Ctrl` `→`
6: Line up	`Ctrl` `E`	<ESC> H `↑`	
7: Line down	`Ctrl` `X`	<ESC> P `↓`	
8: Scroll up	`Ctrl` `W`	_ _ _ _ _ _	
9: Scroll down	`Ctrl` `Z`	_ _ _ _ _ _	
10: Page up	`Ctrl` `R`	<ESC> I	`PgUp`
11: Page down	`Ctrl` `C`	<ESC> Q	`PgDn`
12: To left on line	`Ctrl` `Q` `S`	<ESC> G	`Home`
13: To right on line	`Ctrl` `Q` `D`	<ESC> O	`End`
14: To top of page	`Ctrl` `Q` `E`	<ESC> w	`Ctrl` `Home`
15: To bottom of page	`Ctrl` `Q` `X`	<ESC> u	`Ctrl` `End`
16: To top of file	`Ctrl` `Q` `R`	<ESC> Ctrl-D(+128)	`Ctrl` `PgUp`
17: To end of file	`Ctrl` `Q` `C`	<ESC> v	`Ctrl` `PgDn`
18: To eof w/time/date stamp	`Ctrl` `Q` `0`	_ _ _ _ _ _	
19: To beginning of block	`Ctrl` `Q` `B`	_ _ _ _ _ _	
20: To end of block	`Ctrl` `Q` `K`	_ _ _ _ _ _	
21: To last cursor position	`Ctrl` `Q` `P`	_ _ _ _ _ _	

INSERT & DELETE:

22: Insert mode on/off	`Ctrl` `V`	<ESC> R	`Ins`
23: Insert line	`Ctrl` `N`	_ _ _ _ _ _	
24: Delete line	`Ctrl` `Y`	_ _ _ _ _ _	
25: Delete to end of line	`Ctrl` `Q` `Y`	_ _ _ _ _ _	
26: Delete right word	`Ctrl` `T`	_ _ _ _ _ _	
27: Delete char. under cursor	`Ctrl` `G`	<ESC> S	
28: Delete left character	`Del`	Ctrl-H	`←`
29: Alternative:	_ _ _ _ _ _	_ _ _ _ _ _	

ACTION	SECONDARY COMMAND	PRIMARY COMMAND	PC KEY
BLOCK COMMANDS:			
30: Mark block begin	`Ctrl` `K` `B`	\<ESC\> A	`F7`
31: Mark block end	`Ctrl` `K` `K`	\<ESC\> B	`F8`
32: Mark single word	`Ctrl` `K` `T`		
33: Hide/display block	`Ctrl` `K` `H`	_ _ _ _ _ _	
34: Copy block	`Ctrl` `K` `C`	_ _ _ _ _ _	
35: Move block	`Ctrl` `K` `V`	_ _ _ _ _ _	
36: Delete block	`Ctrl` `K` `Y`	_ _ _ _ _ _	
37: Read block from disk	`Ctrl` `K` `R`	_ _ _ _ _ _	
38: Write block to disk	`Ctrl` `K` `W`	_ _ _ _ _ _	
39: Sort block	`Ctrl` `K` `S`	_ _ _ _ _ _	
40: Print block	`Ctrl` `K` `P`	_ _ _ _ _ _	
41: Paste block	`Ctrl` `K` `E`	_ _ _ _ _ _	
MISC. EDITING COMMANDS:			
42: Save note file	`Ctrl` `K` `D`	\<ESC\> \<	`F2`
43: Tab	`Ctrl` `I`	_ _ _ _ _ _	`Ki`
44: Repeat last find	`Ctrl` `L`	_ _ _ _ _ _	
45: Control character prefix	`Ctrl` `P`	_ _ _ _ _ _	
46: Find	`Ctrl` `Q` `F`	_ _ _ _ _ _	
47: Find & replace	`Ctrl` `Q` `A`	_ _ _ _ _ _	
48: Auto indent off/on	`Ctrl` `Q` `I`	_ _ _ _ _ _	
49: Restore line	`Ctrl` `Q` `L`	_ _ _ _ _ _	
50: Time/date stamp	`Ctrl` `Q` `T`	_ _ _ _ _ _	
51: Graphics on/off	`Ctrl` `Q` `G`	_ _ _ _ _ _	
52: Set right margin	`Ctrl` `O` `R`	_ _ _ _ _ _	
53: Re-format paragraph	`Ctrl` `B`	_ _ _ _ _ _	

Table B-1: Editing Commands PC-Keys

Notepad File Size

As Notepad keeps its text entirely within memory, space must be set aside in memory for it. The default size is 4000 characters, but you may choose a smaller size if you have memory problems, or a larger one if you have lots of memory and want Notepad to work on large files.

Right Margin

The Notepad comes with the right margin set for column 65. If you enter text beyond that column, it will automatically 'wrap around' and continue on the next line. You can use this installation to set another margin. If you want to disable word wrap, just set the right margin to 250.

The right margin can also be changed when you use the Notepad: press [Ctrl] [O] [R], and enter a new value. You can even save the new setting of the right margin from the Sidekick Setup: press [Alt] [S] [F3] to save *Window Setup*.

Dialer

Modem Type
Sidekick comes pre-installed for a Hayes 300/1200/1200B modem. This installation lets you choose from a list of other popular modems and dialers.

Telephone Number Format
Sidekick uses certain conventions to distinguish a telephone number from other numbers on the screen or in your telephone directory. By default, a number must meet the following specifications to qualify as a phone number:

Minimum number of digits: **6**
Required character: - ( )

The installation program lets you change these values if they don't fit the format of your phone numbers.

Minimum number of digits

Set this value to the shortest telephone number you are likely to encounter. The allowable range is 1 through 80.

Required character

This defines which character(s) **must** be present in a phone number. If more than one character is specified, only one of them need be present. Specify up to ten characters as needed. Default required characters are: - ( )

Modem Port

Before using the dialer, you must use SKINST to tell Sidekick on which port your modem is installed. The PC may have two serial communications ports (COM1: and COM2:). Simply press ① or ② depending on which port your modem uses. If you don't know this, check with the person who installed your modem. Pressing ⓪ means that no modem is installed.

If you don't have a modem, you can still use the Dialer as a 'Rolodex' file—but it won't dial for you.

Colors

The cOlor installation lets you change the colors and b/w and mono-chrome attributes used for window frames and text in Sidekick. The standard colors and attributes have been carefully chosen to provide clear and informative screen images with standard IBM video controllers and monitors.

Some other controllers and monitors, however, may display colors differently, and you may then use this installation to design the Sidekick windows to look their best on your particular hardware.

The color installation screen has several windows:

```
┌──────────◀ INSTRUCTIONS ▶──────────┐  ┌──────────────┐
│ Use █ and █ keys to select window. Then choose colors │  │ForegroundFor │
│ for FOREGROUND, BACKGROUND, and FRAME from table below.│  │egroundForegr │
│ Enter the number of the color you want and press ◄┘.   │  │oundForegroun │
│ You will immediately see the effect in the sample window│  │dForegroundFo │
│ to the right or on the command line below.             │  │BackgroundBac │
└────────────────────────────────────────────────────────┘  │kgroundBackgr │
                                                             │oundBackgroun │
      1   2   3   4   5   6   7      9  10  11  12  13  14  15│dBackgroundBa │
   16  17  18  19  20  21  22  23  24  25  26  27  28  29  30  31│ForegroundFor │
   32  33  34  35  36  37  38  39  40  41  42  43  44  45  46  47│egroBackgregr │
   48  49  50  51  52  53  54  55  56  57  58  59  60  61  62  63│oundroundroun │
   64  65  66  67  68  69  70  71  72  73  74  75  76  77  78  79│dForegroundFo │
   80  81  82  83  84  85  86  87  88  89  90  91  92  93  94  95│─────FRAME─── │
   96  97  98  99 100 101 102 103 104 105 106 107 108 109 110 111│              │
  ▓112▓113 114 115 116 117 118 119▓120▓121 122 123 124 125 126 127│ FO  │  BA    │
                                                             └──────────────┘
 █-█-select window  F2-exit and update  Esc-exit without change
```

```
┌─────────────────────────────────────────────────────────────┐
│ FOREGROUND: ▓15▓        BACKGROUND:  7        FRAME:  15       │
│                                                               │
│ Command line  ▓Main window▓  Help       Notepad  Calculator  Calendar │
│ Appointments   Dialer        Ascii table  Setup   File window │
└─────────────────────────────────────────────────────────────┘
```

Figure B-3: COlor Installation

The bottom window shows the names of Sidekick's windows. When you start installation, the Main Window is selected, and the colors of this window are shown in the sample window in the upper right corner.

Press ⏵ or ⏴ to select other windows. The sample window will display the colors of the frame and foreground/background text of each window as you move along.

The top line of the bottom window shows the numeric value of the colors as they are now. To change a color, simply enter another number and press ◄┘. The change will immediately show in the sample window. The table in the middle of the screen will help you to choose colors which show clearly and pleasantly on your screen.

You press ◄┘ to move among the FOREGROUND, BACKGROUND, and FRAME fields.

The table shows color numbers from 1 through 127 (0 is black on black, so you can't see it, and you can't install it either). Numbers 129 through 255 repeat these colors, but **blinking**. It's probably not very useful, but you **can** choose a color to blink by adding 128 to the number in the table.

When you select **Command line**, the sample window disappears, and the installation program's own command line serves as an example of Sidekick's command line. You should note that the colors of the command line are also used by the horizontal bar in the Main Selection Window.

When you are finished re-coloring Sidekick, just press `F2`, and your changes are saved in all Sidekick .COM files on your disk. If you want to leave without saving your changes, just press `Esc`.

Notice that the changes only affect the Sidekick files on disk. The Sidekick you may already have loaded is not installed; you must re-start it to see the new colors.

We hope you'll have a lot of fun coloring your Sidekick.

Activate Commands

There are two ways to activate Sidekick once it's loaded into memory. You can press:

`Ctrl` `Alt`

or you can press the two `⇧` keys simultaneously.

If one or both of these commands collide with other software, you can change them with this installation. The instructions on the screen will tell you how.

Appendix C
HELP!

This appendix answers the questions that you are most likely to have about Sidekick. So in order to save time—yours as well as ours—please check the following pages if you have any problems.

If you don't find the solution to your problem, please have the following information ready before calling our technical support staff. It will help us answer your question quickly and accurately.

Also, please have your computer ready in front of you when you call for technical support. We often need to step you through specific procedures in order to find a solution to your problem.

Product name and version number

You'll find the version number in the log-on message that is displayed when Sidekick is first loaded and at the top of the setup window.

Computer make and model number

Operating system and version number

To get the DOS version number, type VER ⏎ on the DOS command line.

In order for us to determine the exact setup of your operating environment, it would also be helpful if you have a listing of your AUTOEXEC.BAT and CONFIG.SYS files at hand.

(In)compatibility problems

If your Sidekick problem occurs when you run certain programs, but not with others, please give us the names and version numbers of the software causing the problem.

Other resident programs

Are you using other resident programs such as a RAM disk, a spooler, a keyboard enhancer, etc.? If so, please be sure to follow the instructions given on page 114 for using Sidekick with other resident programs.

If you still have problems, please have a list of the other RAM resident programs, and their version numbers, ready when you call us.

Changing Disks

It most likely becomes **necessary** to change disks while Sidekick is active, especially if you have a floppy disk-based computer.

Please be careful when you change disks! DOS sometimes loses track of what's on your disks when you 'swap' disks, and that can result in partially destroyed files, or even an entirely scrambled disk.

As a precaution, you should therefore press ⌨Ctrl⌨C after you re-insert a disk **before** you write on it.

This assumes that you are at the DOS prompt when you swap disks. **You should never swap disks while you are running an application program** (unless that program tells you to do so, of course—then you are safe).

Don't swap the disks that Sidekick uses unless you see the DOS prompt (for example A>) and then always press ⌨Ctrl⌨C before writing on a newly inserted disk.

Dialer

Sidekick's Dialer requires a Hayes or compatible modem, a PCjr. modem, an AT&T 4000 or a VOAD Keyboard Phone. Other modems may be added to the list. Please check the installation program for an up-to-date list of modems currently supported.

If you have difficulties getting the Dialer to work correctly, there are a few things to check for:

1) Verify that your modem is one of those found on the installation menu. And check 'compatible' modems for true compatibility.

2) Make sure that your modem has been installed correctly with Sidekick. During installation, the Sidekick .COM files must be on the same drive and directory as SKINST.COM in order to be installed correctly.

3) Has the installed version of Sidekick been loaded into memory after installation? SKINST makes changes only on .COM files, not in memory.

4) Double check that the telephone number you are trying to dial is valid. You will hear a buzzing sound if an invalid number is used. This could be caused by any of the following errors:

a. Not enough digits to be a valid phone number.
b. None of the *required characters* present in the number.
c. Illegal characters in the phone number.

If this does not solve your problem, then make sure that the modem is configured correctly at the system level.

Even though your communications software recognizes your modem and dials correctly, your system may still be configured incorrectly.

The following test duplicates the procedure Sidekick uses when it dials a telephone number.

Enter the following commands to DOS (if your modem is on port 2, substitute COM2 for COM1):

```
MODE COM1:300,N,8,1 ⏎
COPY CON COM1: ⏎
ATDT123-4567 ⏎
Ctrl Z ⏎
```

If the telephone number is dialed by your modem, then your system is correctly installed. If not, then please refer to the description of the MODE command in your DOS manual.

Foreign and Semi-graphic Characters

The Notepad will display foreign characters and semi-graphics if you press:

```
Ctrl Q G
```

to activate *Graph* mode. This is very useful, for example, if data that you import from the screen contains frames and other special characters.

You can also 'type' these special characters into the Notepad if you hold down the Alt key and enter the character's decimal ASCII value on the **numeric keypad**.

Note that if you use a keyboard enhancer such as SuperKey, you must press ⬧ Alt instead of Alt .

Let's say you want to enter a lower left corner of a frame, for example. Call up the ASCII table and look for that character. When you find it, you have its decimal value in the second column to the left (under the *D*). The single-line lower left corner is 192.

Now return to the Notepad and hold down Alt while you enter the number 192 **on the numeric keyboard**. Then release Alt . You have about 1.5 seconds to do it before Sidekick's main menu pops up.

Formatting Diskettes

A diskette must be *formatted* before you can copy files to it. If you want to copy Sidekick to a new disk you should therefore first do the following:

On Floppy-disk Computers

Place your system disk in drive A: and log on to that drive by typing:

A: ⏎

Now insert the new disk in drive B: and type

FORMAT B: ⏎

It is important that you remember the drive name in the format command; you may otherwise end up formatting your system disk!!! That will erase all your files, so be careful!

The screen now tells you that FORMAT is ready to go to work:

Insert new diskette for drive B:
and strike any key when ready

Check that it really says **drive B:** before you press a key to start formatting! If it does not, press Ctrl C to stop FORMAT (hold down the Ctrl key and press C). **If you press any other key, you will start formatting**.

If your computer has only one disk drive, you can still use the same commands. The computer will treat that one drive as both A: and B:. Just be **sure** to remove the system disk and insert the new disk before you 'strike any key' to start formatting.

When done, FORMAT will ask if you want to format another disk. You may press Y and repeat the formatting for as many disks as you want, or you may press N to stop FORMAT.

Transferring a DOS System to the Disk

If you want to be able to boot from the new disk, you should include a **/S** in the FORMAT command:

FORMAT B: /S ⏎

The operating system files are then automatically copied from the logged drive to the newly formatted diskette. This will allow you to boot your system and load Sidekick all with the same diskette.

On Fixed-disk Computers

Place the new disk in the floppy drive (drive A:) and type:

FORMAT A: ⏎

It is important that you remember the drive name in the format command; you may otherwise end up formatting your entire fixed disk!!! That would erase ALL your files, so be extremely careful!

The screen now tells you that FORMAT is ready to go to work:

Insert new diskette for drive A:
and strike any key when ready

Check that it really says **drive A:** before you press a key to start formatting! If it doesn't, press Ctrl C to stop FORMAT (hold down the Ctrl key and press C). **If you press any other key, you will start formatting.**

When done, FORMAT asks if you want to format another disk. Press Y to repeat the formatting, or press N to stop FORMAT.

Installation

Appendix B gives a complete description of the installation program SKINST, but here's a quick summary:

Screen Type

Press ⑤ to install the display mode.

By default, Sidekick uses whichever screen mode is active when you load it. This should be adequate for most system configurations.

Be sure you choose a mode setting that is compatible with your hardware. For example: a monochrome adapter must be installed in your computer if the Monochrome mode is chosen.

Monochrome refers to a one-color monitor connected to a monochrome video controller with a 9-pin 'parallel' connection. Examples are the standard IBM monochrome monitor, the Amdek or Taxan monochrome monitors, etc.

If you use a composite monochrome monitor connected to a color adapter, it will use a cable with RCA phono jacks at each end. In that case, choose the B/W (black-and-white) mode.

Some monochrome boards support graphics but should still. be installed as monochrome (Hercules for example).

Notepad Commands

Press ⓒ to customize the Notepad editor.

The Notepad editor comes with all of the WordStar-like commands and many special function keys (arrow keys, Home, End, etc.) already installed. It's a good idea to be familiar with the Notepad editor before attempting to change any of these commands.

Notepad File Size

Press [F] to set the maximum file size.

A certain amount of your computer's memory is set aside for the note file. The default file size is 4,000 characters, so if you get the *File too big* error message when you try to load a file, you should install a larger notepad file.

The maximum size for any note file is 50,000 characters. This can be obtained only with the limited Sidekick (SKN.COM). The full version (SK.COM) limits the note file to around 45,000 characters.

Right Margin

The Notepad comes with the right margin set for column 65. If you enter text beyond that column, it will automatically 'wrap around' and continue on the next line. You can use this installation to set another margin. If you want to disable word wrap, just set the right margin to 250.

The right margin can also be changed when you use the Notepad: press [Ctrl] [O] [R], and enter a new value. You can even save the new setting of the right margin from the Sidekick Setup: press [Alt] [S] [F3] to save *Window Setup*.

Dialer

Press [D] to install the modem in your system.

Sidekick must be told which communications port your modem is connected to. Press [1] if your modem is on the COM1: port, or [2] if it's on COM2:.

Colors

Press [O] to change the colors in the window displays.

The color installation is—ironically—especially useful if you use a B/W monitor. Colors are displayed as various shades of gray (or green, or amber, or whatever) on such monitors, and the actual effect varies widely among different hardware combinations.

The best way to find the most legible shades on your particular computer is to try various combinations and watch the effect in the sample window. When you have a good display for one window you could use that for all windows.

Be sure to press ⟨F2⟩ to save the new color setup before you exit.

Activate Commands

The two standard ways to activate Sidekick once it's loaded into memory:

⟨ Ctrl ⟩⟨ Alt ⟩

or the two ⟨⇧⟩ keys may be changed if one or both of these commands collide with other software.

Quit

Press ⟨Q⟩ to quit the installation program when all changes have been made.

Remember that only the Sidekick .COM files are updated at the end of a SKINST session. If Sidekick is still active in memory at this time, remove it and restart it to make the changes effective.

See how to remove Sidekick from memory on page 11.

Framework

If you activate Sidekick while Framework displays graphics, the screen will turn into a pattern of (possibly blinking) characters that make no sense. This is because Sidekick switches the screen to TEXT mode. Don't worry about that. Sidekick will work as usual, and the screen will return to graphics when you leave Sidekick.

LOTUS 123

You may find that when you bring Sidekick up while in the middle of a LOTUS spreadsheet, your computer makes a chirping sound and Sidekick does not come up.

This is because the LOTUS 123 system is configured by default to expect the data disk in drive B:. If you bring up LOTUS and do **not** have a disk in drive B:, a system error is generated. LOTUS ignores this error condition but Sidekick does not.

Make sure that there is always a disk in drive B: whenever LOTUS is loaded. Better yet, reconfigure the LOTUS system to avoid this error condition.

Symphony

Symphony must be installed for TOGGLED mode, not SHARED mode in order for Sidekick to work correctly.

You may find that when you bring Sidekick up while in the middle of a Symphony spreadsheet, your computer makes a chirping sound and Sidekick does not come up.

This is because Symphony is configured by default to expect the data disk in drive B:. If you bring up Symphony and do **not** have a disk in drive B:, a system error is generated. Symphony ignores this error condition but Sidekick does not.

Make sure that there is always a disk in drive B: whenever Symphony is loaded. Better yet, reconfigure Symphony to avoid this error condition.

If you activate Sidekick while Symphony displays graphics, the screen will turn into a pattern of (possibly blinking) characters that make no sense. This is because Sidekick switches the screen to TEXT mode. Don't worry about that. Sidekick will work as usual, and the screen will return to graphics when you leave Sidekick.

WORD

When using Microsoft's WORD with Sidekick, you should start WORD with the command:

WORD/C [←]

to make WORD use normal character mode instead of graphics.

RAM-resident Programs

If you have any other resident programs in memory besides Sidekick, please be sure to load Sidekick **last**. Examples of other resident programs are RAM-disks, print spoolers, certain communication packages, and keyboard enhancers.

If these other resident programs seem to cause problems, try to re-boot your computer and start Sidekick **without** them.

If that solves the problem, you should now determine which of the other resident programs causes the problem. Do that by including the other resident programs one by one, each time re-booting your computer. Always start Sidekick **after** the other resident programs. When the problem crops up, you have found the program that causes the problem.

Appendix D
Using Sidekick With SuperKey

SuperKey, Borland's keyboard enhancer, allows you to record long sequences of keystrokes in a single key called a *macro*. SuperKey also features file encryption, screen protection, keyboard locking, and much, much more.

SuperKey's macros make it a perfect companion for Sidekick. Let's have a look at some macros that will add to the power of Sidekick.

Call Sidekick With a Single Key

The simplest macro you can make calls or exits Sidekick, just like [Ctrl][Alt], but with a single key. Let's record this macro in [F8]. With SuperKey loaded, press:

[Alt] [=] [F8]
[Alt] [/] [C] [S]
[Alt] [-]

These keystrokes record the *Sidekick command* in the macro, so each time you press [F8], you will either activate or exit Sidekick.

Call Sidekick's Calculator

A little more elaborate macro will not only activate Sidekick, but also invoke one of Sidekick's windows. This macro activates the Calculator:

[Alt] [=] [F7]
[Alt] [/] [C] [S] [Alt] [C]
[Alt] [-]

For convenience, you could have a macro for each of Sidekick's windows, so that you could access each one by pressing just one key.

Make Notes

You are probably already using the Notepad to keep notes. Wouldn't it be nice to have a macro that calls the Notepad, drops the cursor to the end of the file so you can enter your note, and then leaves the Notepad when you press ⏎?

The following macro will do just that:

Automatic Cut And Paste

Suppose you have a number of screen forms from which you want to cut some information and put it into the Notepad. The information could be from an order entry form, a personal database, an accounting form, or anything else.

As an example, let's make a macro that cuts the first eight characters of line three of an order entry form and puts them into the Notepad. This is what you need to do for each form:

1) Call Notepad
2) Invoke import from screen
3) Move two lines down and mark the start of the block
4) Move eight characters right and mark the end of the block
5) Import the block into the Notepad and jump to a new line
6) Exit Notepad
7) Go to the next page in the form

The following SuperKey macro does all seven steps for you—at the touch of one key!

Note that this macro uses `Esc` to leave the Notepad. You can also use SuperKey's *Sidekick command* (the equivalent of `Ctrl` `Alt`) if you like.

By the way, you may have to set SuperKey's *Playback delay* to 1 when you play back this macro.

These have been just a few examples of what SuperKey macros can do for your Sidekick. Once you start working on your own, you are certain to discover new and powerful applications.

NOTES

Appendix E
SUBJECT INDEX

H
Help, 14, 105
Hercules board, 95
Hexadecimal numbers, 70
Hide/display block, 53

I
Identifier, 75
Import data from screen, 19, 41
Incompatibility problems, 105
Indent indicator in Notepad, 43
Indentation, 57
Ins, 17, 50
Insert and Delete Commands, 50
Insert indicator in Notepad, 43
Insert line, 17, 51
Insert mode, 50
Insert mode on/off switch, 50
Insert/overwrite characters, 17, 50
Installation, 8, 93, 110

L
Line break, 59, 60
Line indicator in Notepad, 43
Line paste, 55
Line Restore, 64
LOG file, 37
LOTUS 123, 112

M
Margin, 58
Mark block begin/end, 52
Mark single word, 52, 64
Memory size, 10
Minimum number of digits, 102
Miscellaneous Editing
  Commands, 56
  Auto indent off/on, 57
  Control character prefix, 62
  End edit, 56
  Find, 58
  Find and replace, 60
  Graphics on/off, 57
  Repeat last find, 62
  Restore line, 58

Tab, 56
Time/date stamp, 62
Modem Port, 102
Modem Type, 101
Monochrome display, 95
Move block, 53
Move window, 15
Multiple-display adapter, 95

N
Non copy-protected Sidekick, 6
Note File, 81
Note file name, 17, 40, 43
Notepad, 16
Notepad Commands, 97, 110 Ctrl-K-B, 19
Notepad File Size, 20, 42, 101, 111
Notepad vs. the TURBO Pascal Editor, 66
Notepad vs. WordStar, 63

O
OOPS!, 58
Open window, 23
Overwrite/insert, 17, 50

P
Page breaks, 64
Paradise multi-display card, 95
Paste Block, 65, 67
Paste delay factor, 56, 83
Paste key, 54
Paste speed, 56, 83
Pasting Numbers From the Calculator, 25, 70
Path, 18, 41, 83
Pattern, 18, 41
Pause in dialing, 76
Phone directory file, 30, 75
Phone number, 76
Print block, 54, 65, 66
Printer control characters, 62
Print spoolers, 8

Borland
Software

BORLAND
I N T E R N A T I O N A L   *4585 Scotts Valley Drive, Scotts Valley, CA 95066*

REFLEX® THE DATABASE MANAGER

The high-performance database manager that's so advanced it's easy to use!

Lets you organize, analyze and report information faster than ever before! If you manage mailing lists, customer files, or even your company's budgets—Reflex is the database manager for you!

Reflex is the acclaimed, high-performance database manager you've been waiting for. Reflex extends database management with business graphics. Because a picture is often worth a 1000 words, Reflex lets you extract critical information buried in mountains of data. With Reflex, when you look, you see.

The **REPORT VIEW** allows you to generate everything from mailing labels to sophisticated reports. You can use database files created with Reflex or transferred from Lotus 1-2-3,® dBASE,® PFS: File,® and other applications.

Reflex: The Critics' Choice

". . . if you use a PC, you should know about Reflex . . . may be the best bargain in software today."
Jerry Pournelle, BYTE

"Everyone agrees that Reflex is the best-looking database they've ever seen."
Adam B. Green, InfoWorld

"The next generation of software has officially arrived."
Peter Norton, PC Week

Reflex: don't use your PC without it!
Join hundreds of thousands of enthusiastic Reflex users and experience the power and ease of use of Borland's award-winning Reflex.

Suggested Retail Price: $149.95 (not copy protected)

Minimum system configuration: IBM PC, XT, AT, and true compatibles. 384K RAM minimum. IBM Color Graphics Adapter, Hercules Monochrome Graphics CArd, or equivalent. PC-DOS (MS-DOS) 2.0 or greater. Hard disk and mouse optional. Lotus 1-2-3, dBASE, or PFS: File optional.

BORLAND INTERNATIONAL

Reflex is a trademark of Borland/Analytica Inc. Lotus 1-2-3 is a registered trademark of Lotus Development Corporation. dBASE is a registered trademark of Ashton-Tate. PFS: File is a registered trademark of Software Publishing Corporation. IBM, XT, AT, and IBM Color Graphics Adapter are registered trademarks of International Business Machines Corporation. Hercules Graphics Card is a trademark of Hercules Computer Technology. MS-DOS is a registered trademark of Microsoft Corp.   Copyright 1987 Borland International   BOR 0066C

REFLEX: THE WORKSHOP™

Includes 22 "instant templates" covering a broad range of business applications (listed below). Also shows you how to customize databases, graphs, crosstabs, and reports. It's an invaluable analytical tool and an important addition to another one of our best sellers, Reflex: The Database Manager.

Fast-start tutorial examples:

Learn Reflex® as you work with practical business applications. The Reflex Workshop Disk supplies databases and reports large enough to illustrate the power and variety of Reflex features. Instructions in each Reflex Workshop chapter take you through a step-by-step analysis of sample data. You then follow simple steps to adapt the files to your own needs.

22 practical business applications:

Workshop's 22 "instant templates" give you a wide range of analytical tools:

Administration
- Scheduling Appointments
- Planning Conference Facilities
- Managing a Project
- Creating a Mailing System
- Managing Employment Applications

Sales and Marketing
- Researching Store Check Inventory
- Tracking Sales Leads
- Summarizing Sales Trends
- Analyzing Trends

Production and Operations
- Summarizing Repair Turnaround

- Tracking Manufacturing Quality Assurance
- Analyzing Product Costs

Accounting and Financial Planning
- Tracking Petty Cash
- Entering Purchase Orders
- Organizing Outgoing Purchase Orders
- Analyzing Accounts Receivable
- Maintaining Letters of Credit
- Reporting Business Expenses
- Managing Debits and Credits
- Examining Leased Inventory Trends
- Tracking Fixed Assets
- Planning-Commercial Real Estate Investment

Whether you're a newcomer learning Reflex basics or an experienced "power user" looking for tips, Reflex: The Workshop will help you quickly become an expert database analyst.

Minimum system configuration: IBM PC, AT, and XT, and true compatibles. PC-DOS (MS-DOS) 2.0 or greater. 384K RAM minimum. Requires Reflex: The Database Manager, and IBM Color Graphics Adapter, Hercules Monochrome Graphics Card or equivalent.

 **BORLAND** *INTERNATIONAL*

Suggested Retail Price: $69.95
(not copy protected)

Reflex is a registered trademark and Reflex: The Workshop is a trademark of Borland/Analytica, Inc. IBM, AT, and XT are registered trademarks of International Business Machines Corp. Hercules is a trademark of Hercules Computer Technology. MS-DOS is a registered trademark of Microsoft Corp. Copyright 1987 Borland International

BOR 0088B

TURBO PASCAL®

VERSION 4.0

Turbo Pascal 4.0 has all the features

Turbo Pascal 4.0 has all the features of Turbo Pascal 3.0, *plus* an amazing compilation speed of 27,000 lines per minute,* support for programs larger than 64K, a library of powerful standard units, separate compilation, and much more.

The single-pass, native code compiler offers improved code generation, smart linking to remove unused code from your programs, built-in project management, separate compilation using units, output screen saved in a window, MAP files for use with standard debuggers, a command-line version of the compiler and MAKE utility, and built-in support for 8087/80287/80387 math coprocessors.

All these advanced features, plus the integrated programming environment, online help, and Borland's famous pull-down menus, make Turbo Pascal 4.0 the high-speed, high-performance development tool every programmer hopes for.

Built-in editor

An improved, full-screen editor for editing, compiling, and finding and correcting errors from inside the integrated development environment. Supports 25, 43, and 50 lines per screen, tabs, colors, and new command installation.

Interactive error detection

The compiler instantly locates errors, automatically activates the editor, and shows you the location of the error in the source code.

Pick list

Lets you pick a file from a list of the last eight files loaded into the editor and opens it at the exact spot where you last edited the file. It even remembers your last search string and search options.

Free MicroCalc spreadsheet

A new and improved version of the full-fledged spreadsheet included on your Turbo Pascal disk, absolutely free! You get the complete, revised source code, ready to compile and run.

Compatibility with Turbo Pascal 3.0

A conversion program and compatibility units help you convert all your 3.0 programs to 4.0.

Other Technical Features:

□ Several powerful standard units (*System Dos, Crt,* and *Graph*)
□ Device-independent graphics support for CGA, MCGA, EGA, VGA, Hercules, AT&T 6300, and IBM 3270 PC
□ Extended data types, including *LongInt*
□ Optional range- and stack-checking; short-circuit Boolean expression evaluation
□ Support for inline statements, inline macros, and powerful assembly language interface
□ Faster software-only floating point; toggle switch for 80x87 support including *Single, Double, Extended,* and *Comp* IEEE reals (with numeric coprocessor)
□ Automatic execution of initialization and exit code for each unit
□ Nested include files up to 8 levels deep, including main module and units
□ Operating system calls and interrupts
□ Interrupt procedure support for ISRs
□ Variable and value typecasting
□ Shell to DOS transfer

Minimum system requirements: For the IBM PS/2™ and the IBM® and Compaq® families of personal computers and all 100% compatibles. Integrated environment: 384K; command line: 256K; one floppy drive.
*Run on an 8MHz IBM AT

Suggested retail price $99.95
(not copy protected)

TURBO PROLOG™
TOOLBOX

Enhances Turbo Prolog with more than 80 tools and over 8,000 lines of source code

Turbo Prolog, the natural language of Artificial Intelligence, is the most popular AI package in the world with more than 100,000 users. Our new Turbo Prolog Toolbox extends its possibilities.

The Turbo Prolog Toolbox enhances Turbo Prolog—our 5th-generation computer programming language that brings supercomputer power to your IBM PC and compatibles—with its more than 80 tools and over 8,000 lines of source code that can be incorporated into your programs, quite easily.

Turbo Prolog Toolbox features include:

- ☑ Business graphics generation: boxes, circles, ellipses, bar charts, pie charts, scaled graphics
- ☑ Complete communications package: supports XModem protocol
- ☑ File transfers from Reflex,® dBASE III,® Lotus 1-2-3,® Symphony®
- ☑ A unique parser generator: construct your own compiler or query language
- ☑ Sophisticated user-interface design tools
- ☑ 40 example programs
- ☑. Easy-to-use screen editor: design your screen layout and I/O
- ☑ Calculated fields definition
- ☑ Over 8,000 lines of source code you can incorporate into your own programs

---

Suggested Retail Price: $99.95 (not copy protected)

Minimum system configuration: IBM PC, XT, AT or true compatibles. PC-DOS (MS-DOS) 2.0 or later. Requires Turbo Prolog 1.10 or higher. Dual-floppy disk drive or hard disk. 512K.

Turbo Prolog Toolbox and Turbo Prolog are trademarks of Borland International, Inc. Reflex is a registered trademark of Borland/Analytica, Inc. dBASE III is a registered trademark of Ashton-Tate. Lotus 1-2-3 and Symphony are registered trademarks of Lotus Development Corp. IBM, XT, and AT are registered trademarks of International Business Machines Corp. MS-DOS is a registered trademark of Microsoft Corp.

BOR 0240

TURBO BASIC®

The high-speed BASIC you've been waiting for!

You probably know us for our Turbo Pascal® and Turbo Prolog.® Well, we've done it again! We've created Turbo Basic, because BASIC doesn't have to be slow.

If BASIC taught you how to walk, Turbo Basic will teach you how to run!

With Turbo Basic, your only speed is "Full Speed Ahead"! Turbo Basic is a complete development environment with an *amazingly fast compiler*, an *interactive editor* and a *trace debugging system*. And because Turbo Basic is also compatible with BASICA, chances are that you already know how to use Turbo Basic.

Turbo Basic ends the basic confusion

There's now one standard: Turbo Basic. And because Turbo Basic is a Borland product, the price is right, the quality is there, and the power is at your fingertips. Turbo Basic is part of the fast-growing Borland family of programming languages we call the "Turbo Family." And hundreds of thousands of users are already using Borland's languages. So, welcome to a whole new generation of smart PC users!

Free spreadsheet included with source code!

Yes, we've included MicroCalc,™ our sample spreadsheet, complete with source code. So you can get started right away with a "real program." You can compile and run it "as is," or modify it.

A technical look at Turbo Basic

- ☑ Full recursion supported
- ☑ Standard IEEE floating-point format
- ☑ Floating-point support, with full 8087 coprocessor integration. Software emulation if no 8087 present
- ☑ Program size limited only by available memory (no 64K limitation)
- ☑ EGA, CGA, MCGA and VGA support
- ☑ Full integration of the compiler, editor, and executable program, with separate windows for editing, messages, tracing, and execution
- ☑ Compile and run-time errors place you in source code where error occurred
- ☑ Access to local, static and global variables
- ☑ New long integer (32-bit) data type
- ☑ Full 80-bit precision
- ☑ Pull-down menus
- ☑ Full window management

Suggested Retail Price: $99.95 (not copy protected)

Minimum system configuration: IBM PC, AT, XT, PS/2 or true compatibles. 320K. One floppy drive. PC-DOS (MS-DOS) 2.0 or later.

 **BORLAND** *INTERNATIONAL*

TURBO BASIC®
DATABASE TOOLBOX™

With the Turbo Basic Database Toolbox you can build your own powerful, professional-quality database programs. And like all other Borland Toolboxes, it's advanced enough for professional programmers yet easy enough for beginners.

Three ready-to-use modules

The Toolbox enhances your programming with three problem-solving modules:

Turbo Access quickly locates, inserts, or deletes records in a database using B+ trees—the fastest method for finding and retrieving database information. (Source code is included.)

Turbo Sort uses the *Quicksort* method to sort data on single items or on multiple keys. Features virtual memory management for sorting large data files. (Commented source code is on disk.)

TRAINER is a demonstration program that graphically displays how B+ trees work. You can key in sample records and see a visual index of B+ trees being built.

Free sample database

Included is a free sample database with source code. Just compile it, and it's ready to go to work for you—you can use it as is or customize it. You can search the database by keywords or numbers, update records, or add and delete them, as needed.

Saves you time and money

If you're a professional programmer writing software for databases or other applications where search-and-sort capabilities are important, we can save you time and money. Instead of writing the same tedious but essential routines over and over again, you can simply include any of the Toolbox's modules in your own compiled programs.

Technical Features

- ☑ Maximum number of files open: 15 files, or 7 data sets
- ☑ Maximum file size: 32 Mb
- ☑ Maximum record size: 32K
- ☑ Maximum number of records: +2 billion
- ☑ Maximum field size: 32K
- ☑ Maximum key size: 128 bytes
- ☑ Maximum number of keys: +2 billion

Suggested Retail Price: $99.95   (not copy protected)

Minimum system requirements: For the IBM PS/2 and the IBM* and Compaq* families of personal computers and all 100% compatibles, running Turbo Basic 1.0. PC-DOS (MS-DOS*) 2.0 or later. Memory: 640K.

BORLAND
INTERNATIONAL

BOR 0384A

TURBO BASIC®
EdiTur TuuLbuX™

With Turbo Basic we gave you the fastest BASIC around. Now the Turbo Basic Editor Toolbox will help you build your own superfast editor to incorporate into your Turbo Basic programs. We provide all the editing routines. You plug in the features you want!

Two sample editors with source code

To demonstrate the tremendous power of the Toolbox, we've included two sample editors with complete source code:

FirstEd. A complete editor with windows, block commands, and memory-mapped screen routines, all ready to include in your programs.

MicroStar™: A full-blown text editor with a pull-down menu user interface and all the standard features you'd expect in any word processor. Plus features other word processors can't begin to match:

☑ RAM-based editor for superfast editing

☑ View and edit up to eight windows at a time

☑ Support for line, stream, and column block mode

☑ Instant paging, scrolling, and text display

☑ Up to eight hidden buffers at a time to edit, swap, and call text from

☑ Multitasking to let you print in the "background"

☑ Keyboard installation for customizing command keys

☑ Custom designing of colors for text, windows, menus, and status line

☑ Support for DOS functions like Copy file, Delete file, Change directory, and Change logged drive

Build the word processor of your choice!

We give you easy-to-install modules. Use them to build yourself a full-screen editor with pull-down menus, and make it work as fast as most word processors—without having to spend hundreds of dollars!

Source code for everything in the Toolbox is provided. Use any of its features in your own Turbo Basic programs or in programs you develop for others. You don't even have to pay royalties!

Suggested Retail Price: $99.95 (not copy protected)

Minimum system requirements: For the IBM PS/2™ and the IBM® and Compaq® families of personal computers and all 100% compatibles running Turbo Basic 1.0. PC-DOS (MS-DOS®) 2.0 or greater. Memory: 640K.

TURBO C®

A complete interactive development environment

With Turbo C, you can expect what only Borland delivers: Quality, Speed, Power and Price. And with its compilation speed of more than 7000 lines a minute, Turbo C makes everything else look like an exercise in slow motion.

Turbo C: The C compiler for both amateurs and professionals

If you're just beginning and you've "kinda wanted to learn C," now's your chance to do it the easy way. Turbo C's got everything to get you going. If you're already programming in C, switching to Turbo C will considerably increase your productivity and help make your programs both smaller and faster.

Turbo C: a complete interactive development environment

Like Turbo Pascal® and Turbo Prolog,™ Turbo C comes with an interactive editor that will show you syntax errors right in your source code. Developing, debugging, and running a Turbo C program is a snap!

Technical Specifications

☑ **Compiler:** One-pass compiler generating native in-line code, linkable object modules and assembler. The object module format is compatible with the PC-DOS linker. Supports small, medium, compact, large, and huge memory model libraries. Can mix models with near and far pointers. Includes floating point emulator (utilizes 8087/80287 if installed).

☑ **Interactive Editor:** The system includes a powerful, interactive full-screen text editor. If the compiler detects an error, the editor automatically positions the cursor appropriately in the source code.

☑ **Development Environment:** A powerful "Make" is included so that managing Turbo C program development is easy. Borland's fast "Turbo Linker" is also included. Also includes pull-down menus and windows. Can run from the environment or generate an executable file.

☑ Links with relocatable object modules created using Borland's Turbo Prolog into a single program.

☑ ANSI C compatible.

☑ Start-up routine source code included.

☑ Both command line and integrated environment versions included.

"Sieve" benchmark (25 iterations)

	Turbo C	Microsoft® C	Lattice C
Compile time	**3.89**	16.37	13.90
Compile and link time	**9.94**	29.06	27.79
Execution time	**5.77**	9.51	13.79
Object code size	**274**	297	301
Price	**$99.95**	$450.00	$500.00

Benchmark run on a 6 Mhz IBM AT using Turbo C version 1.0 and the Turbo Linker version 1.0; Microsoft C version 4.0 and the MS overlay linker version 3.51; Lattice C version 3.1 and the MS object linker version 3.05.

Suggested Retail Price: $99.95* (not copy protected)   *Introductory offer good through July 1, 1987

Minimum system configuration: IBM PC, XT, AT and true compatibles. PC-DOS (MS-DOS) 2.0 or later. One floppy drive. 320K.

EUREKA: THE SOLVER™

The solution to your most complex equations—in seconds!

If you're a scientist, engineer, financial analyst, student, teacher, or any other professional working with equations, Eureka: The Solver can do your Algebra, Trigonometry and Calculus problems in a snap.

Eureka also handles maximization and minimization problems, plots functions, generates reports, and saves an incredible amount of time. Even if you're not a computer specialist, Eureka can help you solve your real-world mathematical problems fast, without having to learn numerical approximation techniques. Using Borland's famous pull-down menu design and context-sensitive help screens, Eureka is easy to learn and easy to use—as simple as a hand-held calculator.

$X + exp(X) = 10$ solved instantly instead of eventually!

Imagine you have to "solve for X," where $X + exp(X) = 10$, and you don't have Eureka: The Solver. What you do have is a problem, because it's going to take a lot of time guessing at "X." With Eureka, there's no guessing, no dancing in the dark—you get the right answer, right now. (PS: $X = 2.0705799$, and Eureka solved that one in .4 of a second!)

How to use Eureka: The Solver

It's easy.
1. Enter your equation into the full-screen editor
2. Select the "Solve" command
3. Look at the answer
4. You're done

You can then tell Eureka to
- Evaluate your solution
- Plot a graph
- Generate a report, then send the output to your printer, disk file or screen
- Or all of the above

Some of Eureka's key features

You can key in:
- ☑ A formula or formulas
- ☑ A series of equations—and solve for all variables
- ☑ Constraints (like X has to be $<$ or $= 2$)
- ☑ A function to plot
- ☑ Unit conversions
- ☑ Maximization and minimization problems
- ☑ Interest Rate/Present Value calculations
- ☑ Variables we call "What happens?," like "What happens if I change this variable to 21 and that variable to 27?"

Eureka: The Solver includes

- ☑ A full-screen editor
- ☑ Pull-down menus
- ☑ Context-sensitive Help
- ☑ On-screen calculator
- ☑ Automatic 8087 math co-processor chip support
- ☑ Powerful financial functions
- ☑ Built-in and user-defined math and financial functions
- ☑ Ability to generate reports complete with plots and lists
- ☑ Polynomial finder
- ☑ Inequality solutions

Minimum system configuration: IBM PC, AT, XT, PS/2, Portable, 3270 and true compatibles. PC-DOS (MS-DOS) 2.0 and later. 384K.

Suggested Retail Price: $167.00
(not copy protected)

BORLAND
INTERNATIONAL

SIDEKICK® THE DESKTOP ORGANIZER Release 2.0

Macintosh™

The most complete and comprehensive collection of desk accessories available for your Macintosh!

Thousands of users already know that SideKick is the best collection of desk accessories available for the Macintosh. With our new Release 2.0, the best just got better.

We've just added two powerful high-performance tools to SideKick—Outlook™: The Outliner and MacPlan™: The Spreadsheet. They work in perfect harmony with each other and *while* you run other programs!

Outlook: The Outliner

- It's the desk accessory with more power than a stand-alone outliner
- A great desktop publishing tool, Outlook lets you incorporate both text and graphics into your outlines
- Works hand-in-hand with MacPlan
- Allows you to work on several outlines at the same time

MacPlan: The Spreadsheet

- Integrates spreadsheets and graphs
- Does both formulas and straight numbers
- Graph types include bar charts, stacked bar charts, pie charts and line graphs
- Includes 12 example templates free!
- Pastes graphics and data right into Outlook creating professional memos and reports, complete with headers and footers.

SideKick: The Desktop Organizer, Release 2.0 now includes

- ☑ Outlook: The Outliner
- ☑ MacPlan: The Spreadsheet
- ☑ Mini word processor
- ☑ Calendar
- ☑ PhoneLog
- ☑ Analog clock
- ☑ Alarm system
- ☑ Calculator
- ☑ Report generator
- ☑ Telecommunications (new version now supports XModem file transfer protocol)

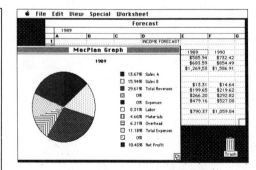

MacPlan does both spreadsheets and business graphs. Paste them into your Outlook files and generate professional reports.

Suggested Retail Price: $99.95 (not copy protected)

Minimum system configurations: Macintosh 512K or Macintosh Plus with one disk drive. One 800K or two 400K drives are recommended. With one 400K drive, a limited number of desk accessories will be installable per disk.

SideKick is a registered trademark and Outlook and MacPlan are trademarks of Borland International, Inc. Macintosh is a trademark of McIntosh Laboratory, Inc. licensed to Apple Computer, Inc. Copyright 1987 Borland International

BOR 0069D

TURBO

PASCAL® MACINTOSH™

The ultimate Pascal development environment

Borland's new Turbo Pascal for the Mac is so incredibly fast that it can compile 1,420 lines of source code in the 7.1 seconds it took you to read this!

And reading the rest of this takes about *5 minutes*, which is plenty of time for Turbo Pascal for the Mac to compile at least *60,000 more lines* of source code!

Turbo Pascal for the Mac does both Windows and "Units"

The *separate* compilation of routines offered by Turbo Pascal for the Mac creates modules called "Units," which can be linked to any Turbo Pascal program. This "modular pathway" gives you "pieces" which can then be integrated into larger programs. You get a more efficient use of memory and a reduction in the time it takes to develop large programs.

Turbo Pascal for the Mac is so compatible with Lisa® that they should be living together

Routines from Macintosh Programmer's Workshop Pascal and Inside Macintosh can be compiled and run with only the subtlest changes. Turbo Pascal for the Mac is also compatible with the Hierarchical File System of the Macintosh.

The 27-second Guide to Turbo Pascal for the Mac

- Compilation speed of more than 12,000 lines per minute
- "Unit" structure lets you create programs in modular form
- Multiple editing windows—up to 8 at once
- Compilation options include compiling to disk or memory, or compile and run
- No need to switch between programs to compile or run a program
- Streamlined development and debugging
- Compatibility with Macintosh Programmer's

- Workshop Pascal (with minimal changes)
- Compatibility with Hierarchical File System of your Mac
- Ability to define default volume and folder names used in compiler directives
- Search and change features in the editor speed up and simplify alteration of routines
- Ability to use all available Macintosh memory without limit
- "Units" included to call all the routines provided by Macintosh Toolbox

---

Suggested Retail Price: $99.95* (not copy protected)

*Introductory price expires July 1, 1987

Minimum system configuration: Macintosh 512K or Macintosh Plus with one disk drive.

 **BORLAND** *INTERNATIONAL*

Turbo Pascal and SideKick are registered trademarks of Borland International, Inc. and Reflex is a registered trademark of Borland/Analytica, Inc. Macintosh is a trademark of McIntosh Laboratories, Inc. licensed to Apple Computer with its express permission. Lisa is a registered trademark of Apple Computer, Inc. Inside Macintosh is a copyright of Apple Computer, Inc. Copyright 1987 Borland International BOR 0167A

TURBO PASCAL TOOLBOX™
NUMERICAL METHODS

Turbo Pascal Numerical Methods Toolbox for the Macintosh implements the latest high-level mathematical methods to solve common scientific and engineering problems. Fast.

So every time you need to calculate an integral, work with Fourier transforms, or incorporate any of the classical numerical analysis tools into your programs, you don't have to reinvent the wheel, because the Numerical Methods Toolbox is a complete collection of Turbo Pascal routines and programs that gives you applied state-of-the-art math tools. It also includes two graphics demo programs that use least-square and Fast Fourier Transform routines to give you the picture along with the numbers.

The Turbo Pascal Numerical Methods Toolbox is a must if you're involved with any type of scientific or engineering computing on the Macintosh. Because it comes with complete source code, you have total control of your application at all times.

What Numerical Methods Toolbox will do for you:

- Find solutions to equations
- Interpolations
- Calculus: numerical derivatives and integrals
- Matrix operations: inversions, determinants, and eigenvalues

- Differential equations
- Least-squares approximations
- Fourier transforms
- Graphics

Five free ways to look at Least-Squares Fit!

As well as a free demo of Fast Fourier Transforms, you also get the Least-Squares Fit in five different forms—which gives you five different methods of fitting curves to a collection of data points. You instantly get the picture! The five different forms are

1. Power
2. Exponential
3. Logarithm
4. 5-term Fourier
5. 5-term Poynomial

They're all ready to compile and run as is.

Suggested Retail Price: $99.95 (not copy protected)

Minimum system requirements: Macintosh 512K, Macintosh Plus, SE, or II, with one 800K disk drive (or two 400K).

BORLAND
INTERNATIONAL

Borland
Software
ORDER TODAY

BORLAND INTERNATIONAL

4585 Scotts Valley Drive   Scotts Valley, California   95066

To Order By Credit Card, Call (800) 255-8008

In California call (800) 742-1133

In Canada call (800) 237-1136